Mommy Magic

The Magic of Life Series

A series of books to help put a little more magic
into every aspect of your life!
www.TheMagicofLifeSeries.com

Future books in the Magic of Life Series:

*Daddy Magic • Marriage Magic • Music Magic
Pet Magic • Teacher Magic • Teen Magic
Cooking Up Some Magic • The Magic of Hope and
The Magic of Friendship*

Other books by Adria Manary

*Kennedys—The Next Generation
Touched by a Rainbow (with Catherine Burnett)
Kids Hollywood Magic (with Phyllis Henson)*

Mommy Magic

Creative Activities and Inspiring Stories to Deepen the Bond with Your Child

Adria Manary

Tendril Press

DENVER, COLORADO

www.TheMagicofLifeSeries.com

Send *The Magic of Life* your stories and comments, enter *The Magic of Life* contests, utilize the resources and get updates on where Adria is speaking next. *The Magic of Life* looks forward to hearing from you!

Third Edition Published by Tendril Press™ 2011
© 2011 All Rights Reserved
www.TendrilPress.com
PO Box 441110
Aurora, CO 80044
303.696.9227

ISBN 978-0-9841587-9-0 Paper

Library of Congress Control Number: 2011925185

Individual Sales. This book is available through most bookstores or can be ordered directly from the publisher. Quantity Sales. Special discounts are available on quantity purchases by corporations, associations, and others. For details, contact the "Special Sales Department" at the publisher's address above.

Printed in the United States of America
10 9 8 7 6 5 4 3 2 1

Cover Design: Karin Hoffman
Cover Photo: Shutterstock

Art Direction, Book Design and Cover Design © 2011.
All Rights Reserved by

A J Images Inc.,
www.AJImagesInc.com — 303•696•9227
Info@AJImagesInc.com

To my delightful and precious children,
Chase, Dane, Astra and Josh,
and to my incredibly loving,
supportive and talented husband, Joel.

The family is a haven in a heartless world.

—Christopher Lasch

Contents

Mommy Magic
Adria Manary

Foreword

*I*t may seem out of place for a father to be writing the foreword to a book for mothers...but I asked for the honor. I did so because I am blessed with five beautiful, healthy, respectful, caring children, and I deeply understand and appreciate the awesome and often difficult job that my wife did in raising them. Of course it was a team effort and I am an extremely involved dad. In fact, I look forward to writing my own story in Daddy Magic! However, I believe that it is the mother who is the heart of the home and it is books like this one that help them to create the kind of loving and enchanting environment that we all want for our children.

Adria has truly captured the magic of a mother's love within these pages and I suggest you keep a box of tissues handy as you read. Just as important, however, she has created an exceptionally useful resource that all mothers can use on a daily basis. The testimonials within are only a sampling of the rave reviews that this book has received from moms who have deemed this book a "must have" for their library.

As one newspaper headline so aptly put it, "MOMMY MAGIC Casts a Spell of Love." Now in its third edition, I am happy to be the one to introduce you to the sound advice, fun and practical activities, encouraging words, personal stories and moving poetry that will support and comfort you on your parenting quest.

— Richard Paul Evans,
#1 New York Times bestselling author of *The Christmas Box*

Mommy Magic
Adria Manary

Preface
What is the Magic?

It was one of those landmark days when nothing could go wrong. The day began with our regular "morning hugs" and my boys got into the bathtub without whining. There were no spills at breakfast, my little girl and I played diving Barbie in the tub for an hour, and I still got everything done I wanted to get done, while my older ones were at school. As a bonus, when I picked them up...they were full of stories to tell without my usual prodding...and they had NO HOMEWORK!

On the way home, we stopped at the grocery store. They all rode in one of those great shopping carts with the red seats and steering wheels in the front. In addition, I could let them get most of the things they wanted since they were reasonable requests. This made for a fun shopping day!

Since they were so good in the store, their reward was to stop for ice cream. I enjoyed a hot fudge sundae as they laughed and gobbled down their own interesting concoctions. I'll never understand how you get bubble gum into ice cream and why you're allowed to swallow it, but my youngest thought it was the best ice cream she had ever tasted. The boys' combinations were too strange to describe. Of course, these are the same boys who mix every kind of soft drink into one cup when they are allowed to get their own at a "make it yourself" soda fountain. We stole each other's cherries, tasted each other's specialties and got spots on our clothes...including mine. But that was part of the fun.

The day got better as we hit the park and finally arrived home to find Daddy already in the living room—an unexpected grand finale to an already perfect day. Plus, dinner was in the oven! The evening was warmed by loving hearts and a tearjerker movie, topped off by a glowing fire. Some "magic dust" made the fire even more engaging as we tossed it into the flames, which turned into every color of the rainbow. One by one, everyone seemed to be drifting off into dreamland...including my husband.

As I stroked the children's hair I tried to explain what a wonderful time we'd had, but I struggled to find the words to describe the beauty of the day. At that moment my six year old snuggled up as close as he could possibly get and said, "It was because of the magic, Mommy."

"What kind of magic are you talking about, sweetheart?" I asked.

"The magic that's called MOMMY!" he said.

The words stood still in my heart as his eyes gazed into mine. Any of Warhol's "fifteen minutes of fame" could never have compared with this. Tears welled up in my eyes and I couldn't respond, so he continued, "you make things magic for us, Mommy. And I like it!"

I realized at that moment, the magic he was referring to was the everyday environment a mother is responsible for creating around her child. My mother used to tell me she wished she could put me in a magic bubble that would protect me from the hurts of the outside world. I have often felt the same way about my own children—but I realize the key is to prepare them to deal with the many disappointments life will bring, as well as to teach them to enjoy every miracle of life, and every precious moment we have here. This starts early, as

Mommy Magic
Adria Manary

they watch how you deal with the roller coaster of life. As you show the way by example, and teach them to uphold the precious virtues of life, you are indeed creating an invisible bubble that will surround their hearts and souls, and giving them the tools they will need to become happy, productive, and caring adults.

God's words, "...And the greatest of these is love," resonate in my heart constantly. And showing unconditional love to our children is the greatest gift we can give as parents. Demonstrating that love must be constant and varied, playful and soulful, firm when necessary, kind continually, and patient...always.

The following chapters will offer stories, suggestions, tips and activities that will help you on your ceaseless quest to make the world a brighter place for your child. Some of the ideas will awaken the child within you. Some you will have heard a million times, yet reading them again will prompt you to try them. Some you will never have the desire to try. Some you will have done, but the words will remind you how fun they were and you'll want to do them again. Some you will have never heard of and you'll say to yourself, "Why didn't I think of that!" Some will bring tears to your eyes as you remember your mom doing the same for you. And some will make you laugh. But I can assure you that all of the suggestions come from myself and other moms who have tried them and found them worthwhile.

In addition to sharing ideas that will create special, memorable, fun and loving moments with your children, I will briefly explore the magic that exists through amazing sixth-sense connections between a mother and child. Whether you call it mother's intuition, maternal telepathy, or an angel's whisper—it exists, it is very powerful, and it is fascinating.

To understand the full love, power, and responsibility behind motherhood is awe-inspiring, and I wish you the very best on your unique and miraculous journey.

Mommy Magic
Adria Manary

An Update from the Author

From the miracle of birth, to the mystery of death, there is the MAGIC of LIFE!

I am absolutely thrilled to bring you the first book in my new series, The Magic of Life. The journey through life is as fulfilled and amazing as you choose it to be, and its beginnings are nothing less than miraculous. Having had a miscarriage between my first two children, then researching how and why such a horrible thing could happen, the statistics I found were astonishing. When I read that 1 in 5 pregnancies never come to term, I gained a deeper realization of how precious and delicate life is and have tried my best to appreciate every moment with my children. It is also why I decided that *Mommy Magic* should kick off this series...because the miracle of birth, and the enchantment of childhood—from the parent's point of view as well as the child's— are usually the most cherished and magical times of our lives.

When I originally wrote *Mommy Magic* in 2000, my children were 4, 7 and 10 years old. They are now 16, 19 and 22! In addition, we adopted a 17-year-old boy who had been homeless, and is now 21. Therefore, my family has not only gotten older, but also bigger! When I want to sound older and wiser, I say that the original *Mommy Magic* was written at the turn of the century! Since then, I have spent the majority of my time nurturing the magic of love within my own family, with the dream of spreading that magic to the world through a series of books that would help others to embrace and enhance every aspect of the magic of life, no matter what obstacles got in their way.

As I will illustrate often in the following pages, the best gift you can give your child—in tandem with unconditional love—is your time. Looking at my grown children these days, I can remember how many times older moms would offer some version of the following sage advice:

> "Enjoy these years, because they go by faster than you can possibly imagine."

Well, I am now here to tell you how TRUE that statement is. It seems like yesterday when I welcomed each one of my biological children into the world. As much as I cherish their younger years, I also want to share with you how precious each phase of their lives has been. As children grow older, it becomes more and more evident that what you put into the relationship shapes their destinies.

It is my deepest hope that this book will help you make the most of every priceless moment with your children, as well as encourage and inspire you on those days when those usually darling little people seem to bring more stress than delight! If we all remember that life is destined to bring us an abundance of joy, though at times mixed with tears, we can appreciate the balance and celebrate the positive.

With love and laughter,

Adria

Mommy Magic
Adria Manary

Acknowledgments

Although I have given great thought to writing this page, I am always afraid I will leave someone special out. It is an easier task to thank those who were directly involved in the publication of this book, than to go deep into my heart and acknowledge all of the extraordinary people who have played a part in the development of what I have come to believe—and thus shared throughout the pages of this book. I suppose the best way to start is with my highest thanks—to God—for blessing me with such a wonderful family and for the gift of inspiration in writing this book.

From there, I would like to thank my husband Joel, for his love, patience, and inner calm that I need to rest in often; my son Chase, for his love, support, and quiet wisdom; my son Dane, for his love, encouragement, and humor; and my daughter Astra, for her love and constant shining light. I would also like to thank them all collectively, for providing such a large part of the material written in this book! In addition, I would like to thank our adopted son, Josh, who has added a new dimension to our lives and deepened the understanding of the value of family.

I would especially like to thank my mom, for being the original "Mommy Magic" and for her incredible gift of unconditional love;

and my dad for his constant love and never-ending support. Although I can no longer hug them physically, I know they continue to be by my side, as I feel them in my heart every day.

Another very special thanks to "the best brother in the world," my big brother, Brian Hilburn, who has always loved me, protected me, and been there for me at every turn. His wife, Patty, and their wonderful children, Ainsley and Gavin are also my inspirations.

There are many, many friends who come to mind, but the ones who I would like to thank here are those who have been involved and supportive in this particular endeavor, my dearest friends: Patty Schulz, Anne Gallant, Val Acciani, and Chris Sumstine. I love you all dearly.

To my first grade teacher, Catherine Burnett, I offer my heartfelt gratitude. She recognized the artist in me early on, and thirty years after she again ignited my creative spirit when we wrote a book of poetry together called *Touched By A Rainbow*.

My deepest thanks to Pat Pickslay...one of those special souls who can look into your heart and inspire your dreams. Working diligently with him for six months, we produced my music CD, Precious Souls, an experience I shall never forget. He, too, has become a precious and caring friend to me and to my family.

More creative thanks go to Karin Hoffman, founder of Tendril Press, for her dedication to excellence, her patience with me, and her devotion to publishing the series that has been my dream for over ten years. Fortunately for me, she has become a wonderful friend in the process, and has always been on the other end of the phone when I needed a shoulder to cry on.

My love and gratitude also go to the very special members of my extended family, whose love I can always depend on:

Suzan and Ed Schweizer, Alicia Schweizer; Debbie and Brad Thornton, Bradley and Jake; Sally and Ricci DePasquale, "little" Ricci, Joey, Alicia, and John; Elizabeth, Marce and Andrew Scarborough; Ward,

Mommy Magic
Adria Manary

Florence and Alexia Schweizer; Roy and Linda Peterson; Wayne and Kathy Peterson, and their daughter Kathy; Johnny and Michele Peterson; Lisa Bagbey, Devon and Marin; Dawn and Stephen Hall, and Brandon Manary; and Diana Wilson, Julie, Megan, Tracy, and Mike.

And finally, to those who brought the magic of love into my life who may be gone from my sight, but will remain in my heart forever, a humble thank you to my parents, Doris and John Hilburn, Jr., my brother, Dean Hilburn, my grandparents, Edith and Peter Christensen (Deedie and Pop-Pop), and Elizabeth and John Hilburn, Sr., my special aunts, Flora Bowen and Sally Peterson, my mother-in-law, Delores McElhannon and my dear cousin Larry Peterson.

The Magic of a Mother's Love

The magic of a mother's love
Brings harmony and bliss,
It covers like a blanket
And cures booboos with a kiss.

It offers grand protection
From evil that lurks 'round,
It tames the fears of little ones
And turns frowns upside down.

It holds a wealth of wisdom
With gentleness it guides,
It holds the hand when needed
Then lets go with tears of pride.

And though those precious childhood years
In an instant pass,
The love and magic she instills
Will last…and last…and last.

Mommy Magic
Adria Manary

Introduction

———————

I truly believe that when a child is born, God sprinkles a bit of magic into the heart of the mother. Then as the child is laid in her arms, that magic brings feelings of unparalleled love and incredible awe. From that very moment on, the mother and child reconnect as if the baby were still in the womb. What has been a physical connection for nine months magically turns into a heart connection that lasts forever.

As life unfolds, the magic that the mother bestows upon her child becomes a springboard for achievement and a safety net for failure; a treasure trove of hope and the backbone of self-confidence; a blanket to warm the soul and a spark to ignite the spirit.

Outside of the ice rink where my son played hockey is a sculpture of a mother applauding. The earrings that she is wearing are little ice skates and her smile is full of warmth and pride. The quote written beside the statue reads:

A mother's cheers...the driving force behind our achievements.

I think that says it all, as long as we remember that our children's achievements in life will not only include winning a championship game or success in their careers—but also the love of family and friends, the respect of their peers, and peace and harmony in their homes.

Instilled deeply inside of a mother's soul is the desire to create a perfect world for her child. However, as the world becomes more and more demanding, we sometimes let the weight of those pressures erode some of the magic we were blessed with.

It is my hope that this book will help you to keep the magic alive in the midst of the chaotic life that often holds us prisoner. Use it as an occasional reminder—or an "idea a day" guide—to create a strong foundation that the difficulties of life cannot erode. With poems to stir your soul, stories to warm your heart, and hundreds of ideas to keep your children smiling, it was written to provide a helpful reference as you strive to create a more enchanting world for your family.

Every child is born with a loving and joyful soul. It is up to us to nurture and protect it, so it may blossom and leave flowers along the path of their lifetime. I am, and always will be grateful to my mom for loving me unconditionally, making me feel secure, believing in me, supporting me, and reminding me when I had not made the right decision. When she passed away in 1993, I felt completely empty and certainly did not want to suffer the agony of going through her things. However, years later there was a sweet and inspirational moment when I found a book she had obviously treasured in a box that had been packed away for a long time. It was written for the "Future Homemakers of America." Since it was after I had written the first *Mommy Magic* book when I came across her book, you can imagine my amazement when I opened it, and right there on the first page was a poem entitled "Magic." Since I had often referred to my mom as the original "Mommy Magic," I was stunned to see this poem in a book she had read before I was even born! So let us strive to continue the magic of love as we raise the next generation.

Mommy Magic
Adria Manary

Thanks for the Memories...

I feel so blessed to have a place
Where I can take my mind
Whenever tears start flowing
I go far back in time.

To when my mom was here with me
Always by my side
There was no one else who cared as much
Her tears fell when I cried.

I'm thankful for the memories
That fill my mind with joy
The times she took me shopping
Or surprised me with a toy.

The way she never let me leave
Without a hug and kiss
Her constant show of joyful love
Is what I truly miss.

And now I must make certain
That I create a place
Where my children can go and think of me
When they can no longer see my face.

Consider the past and you shall know the future.

– Chinese proverb

Mommy Magic
Adria Manary

Creating Memories

You will find a lot of ideas in this book, but I decided to make this the first chapter because every idea you use will hopefully create good memories for your children. I also thought it would be fun for you to start by conjuring up your own precious memories.

Memories are, of course, created every day...without any conscious effort on our parts. Our experiences are stored away in our brains and when a smell, a song, or a word reminds us of a certain one—memories of the entire instance flood our minds. I've often wondered why bad experiences are more readily remembered than good ones. Maybe it's because they make more of an impression. Imagine ways you can make your children's good experiences more impressionable, and they will have more of those to draw on when hurtful memories are unfortunately added in. Also, repetition is not only the mother of learning, but the mother of memory as well! The more you do something, the deeper ingrained it becomes. So why not put something that smells good on the stove every day, so the house always smells yummy when your children come in the door? Cinnamon toast is a good snack after school—so put cinnamon sticks on the stove one day (the smell lasts longer)—and put rolls in the oven (or bake bread if you're so inclined) the next day...and so on.

The following list is a collection of my own memories, as well of those of many others. My hope is that it will tickle your own memory cells, remind you of things that have been tucked away for a long time, and give you ideas about what memories you want your own children to go through life with. And if you happen not to have been blessed with good memories of your own childhood—this is your chance to prove that history does not have to repeat itself. It is up to you to change your destiny, as well as the destinies of the precious beings you have brought into this world.

The greatest gift you can bestow upon your child is a loving, happy, and secure childhood—for that will be the foundation for how they view the world for the rest of their lives.

Memories of Mom

Cinnamon toast and tea in bed whenever I was sick.

Popsicles in the bathtub.

The first day of school and we both cried.

Saying a prayer together whenever we saw an ambulance
or heard a siren.

Leaving a snack at night for the little people who I thought lived
inside our television set.

The song you sang every morning to wake me up.

Laughing at all of my jokes, and no matter how many times I told you
the one about the elephant on the fence, you still laughed each time!

The special notes you used to put in my lunch box...and later in my care packages at college. I still look for them in my briefcase at times!

❧

Playing for hours under the sprinkler in the front yard—until everyone in the neighborhood had joined in on the fun!
You also provided the popsicles!

❧

Being the hit of the neighborhood by dressing up on Halloween with us and going trick-or-treating.

❧

Family hugs.

❧

Making us feel "rich" on occasion, even when you and Dad were struggling.

❧

The day we all went to that homeless shelter and dished out soup.

❧

The Christmas morning when I heard my new puppy barking!

❧

When I told you the moon was always following me, and you said God put it there to always light my path.

❧

Mommy Magic
Adria Manary

The time we sat on top of the van and watched the sunset over the ocean.

❧

The morning I dressed up in your high heels and glittery sweater, put on your makeup, perfume, and hairspray and woke you with a surprise.

❧

Whenever I missed a line in a play or struck out in a baseball game, you always said my performance had still been spectacular in some way. Like the time you told me that although I struck out, you noticed my swing had become so much stronger that when I connected with the ball next time you were sure it would go over the fence!

❧

Playing school and letting me be the teacher.

❧

Going to camp for the first time and being so excited...until I got to the bus and realized you weren't going with me!

❧

Tea parties with stuffed animals.

❧

When I asked you if I could live with you forever, and you explained how I would grow up and go to college and someday have a family of my own and a house of my own...but that those things would happen far in the future. Then when I told you I would move in next door— you smiled that famous "I love you so much" smile!

❧

The time you got "woozy" blowing up my birthday balloons.

The time I overheard you saying a prayer asking that you would love my future husband and he would love you just as much.

Watching you kiss Daddy every day when he got home and the feeling of security it gave me.

Feeding the ducks at Grandma's.

The party you gave for the whole neighborhood when we first moved...just so I could meet the kids.

Bedtime prayers.

How excited you got when a whistle finally came out after you'd been teaching me how for weeks. Not to mention the first time I made a bubble with bubble gum!

The miraculous way you made the worst night of my life into the most warm and memorable one with you.

Mommy Magic
Adria Manary

The first time I flew on a plane and you asked the pilot if I could sit in the cockpit, and he let me sit in the captain's seat! I'll never forget that moment.

❧

The time I tried on your old costume from your first grade play... it fit and you cried.

❧

Getting a gold coin from the leprechauns every St. Patrick's Day.

❧

The way you always made me feel like a princess.

❧

How I slept with you every night.

❧

The sleigh bells that mysteriously rang outside on Christmas Eve.

❧

The song you made up for me using my name in every other sentence.

❧

NEVER getting library books back on time because I got so attached to them.

❧

The first time I beat you at Ping-Pong.

❧

The first time I beat you at checkers.

The first time I beat you to the phone!

Our many, many shopping trips!

Pet store Saturdays...petting all of the puppies and kitties...and talking to the birds.

The time I took my shoes off after you told me not to and immediately stepped on a bee! Oh, how I appreciated your not scolding me—not realizing you knew I had already had a stinging lesson!

The time we were all supposed to be folding clothes in the living room and you got a bit frustrated with the little amount of work getting done. But instead of getting mad, you put Dad's underwear on your head and said, "If you can't beat 'em, join 'em!"

The famous bubble bath I gave the dog.

When I got lost at the beach...and how long you held me when you finally found me.

Reaching for the sky on the swings when I was little and your encouragement for me to do the same in college!

Your smiling face at school—many, many, many days.

Taking that art class together.

Taking dance together.

Mother-daughter (son) dinners.

Mysterious mail that always had my name on it.

The time you drove 200 miles to bring my favorite pillow to me when I went away to college...a great excuse to see how I was doing!

Lengthy Monopoly games.

The many Halloween outfits that you made for me.

The game I loved when you would take an arm and dad would take a leg, and you both would say, "He's mine...NO...He's MINE. NO, he's MY boy...NO, he's MY BOY!!!"

Ƹ̵̡Ӝ̵̨̄Ʒ

The worst haircut of my entire life—when I refused to go to school for two days...and you let me stay home.

Ƹ̵̡Ӝ̵̨̄Ʒ

Picnics in the backyard.

Ƹ̵̡Ӝ̵̨̄Ʒ

Picnics on the living room floor.

Ƹ̵̡Ӝ̵̨̄Ʒ

Our airport trips to watch the planes take off.

Ƹ̵̡Ӝ̵̨̄Ʒ

Going to the art museum. (I was bored, but I loved being with you, and having lunch in the park afterwards!) It's funny though...I just love art museums now!

Ƹ̵̡Ӝ̵̨̄Ʒ

Planning family vacations.

Ƹ̵̡Ӝ̵̨̄Ʒ

The first time you painted my nails and I wouldn't let you take it off... which you never did... it just wore off and we did it again!

Ƹ̵̡Ӝ̵̨̄Ʒ

Mommy Magic
Adria Manary

The time I got cut from the baseball team and YOU cried.

❧

The vacation when we all went to _____ .
(This is a "fill it in yourself" memory for you!)

❧

The way you would never answer the phone if we were having an important discussion or if I was upset over something.

❧

The stories you would embellish, as Dad would tell them by the fire on special occasions.

❧

Roasting marshmallows and hot dogs on the fire.

❧

The camping trip when we had to use the potato chip can as a toilet.

❧

The infamous day when you "accidentally" bumped my former boyfriend into the community pool because he had made me cry too much.

❧

The night of my first school play when you applauded the most—standing ovation included—even though I only had one word to say during the whole performance.

❧

Surprise visits to Grandmom's and Granddad's.

❧

Picking berries at Aunt _____'s.
(Another fill-in!)

❧

Bike rides on the beach.

❧

That time you made me turn my radio off and just listen to the waves when we were at the beach.

❧

The time we caught about a thousand lightning bugs and kept them in a jar to light up the back porch for awhile. And then you told me we had to let them go because freedom was important to everyone, even animals and insects.

❧

The night we all had to sleep in the car because there were no vacancies for hundreds of miles. It may have been uncomfortable for sleeping, but it was one of the most fun nights the family ever had together!

❧

Helping me bake fifty mini-cookies in my Easy-Bake Oven and taking them around the neighborhood with me.

❧

The many compliments you offered that started my days or evenings out right.

❧

Mommy Magic
Adria Manary

The time you let me eat my birthday cake right out of the pan!!

❧

The time we switched places and I got to be mom for the day.

❧

The look on your face the first weekend I returned home from college freshman year.

❧

The time you wouldn't stop applauding after the spelling bee.

❧

I'll never forget when we found that lost puppy, and how you were so diligent in finding its owner, reminding me how we would feel if we lost our dog.

❧

The way you always tried to include me in conversation, even with your adult friends.

❧

The loan you gave me—and the gift you made of not making me pay it back after the first payment. I guess you just wanted to see if I would be responsible enough to start paying you back.

❧

Reminding me of the miracles of God's creations on a weekly basis. Especially the butterfly that had the most spectacular wings I'd ever seen!

❧

Not getting upset with me the day I came home muddy and sopping wet from playing in every puddle on the way home from school on a warm spring day.

The way you still make me feel... still your pride and joy although I'm all grown up!

Always making my little crisis situations your high priority for problem solving.

The way you were always my best friend. I could always count on you!

The way you let me keep my security blanket even after others said I should give it up. (Do you still have it?)

Tickling me to sleep almost every night.

Making my bedtime stories real with your animation.

Putting my name in the stories that were exciting...making ME the hero!

How you could make an ordinary day into an adventure...even if it was just in our own backyard!

⁂

The time you took us to the Goofy lunch and arranged for him to single our table out.

⁂

Our first trip to "Tomorrowland" at Disneyland. It was so futuristic to think of the possibility of having picture phones, and now we can actually do it! (You've got to get a smart phone, Mom!)

⁂

The tea party with Mary Poppins.

⁂

Always setting the right example—even admitting when you were wrong.

⁂

Falling asleep in your lap as you stroked my hair.

⁂

Constantly reminding me, "I'd never know if I didn't give it a try."

⁂

Teaching me the joy of giving.

⁂

Always, ALWAYS hugging me before we parted. Even if you were just going to the store or I was going to play at a friend's.

⁂

Those constant reminders to think positive and feel positive.

❧

The incredible love in your eyes when you held my first child.

❧

The first time I had Christmas dinner at my house!

❧

How you have always been there for me. In the middle of the night when I was scared as a kid, to the times when I just needed a home-cooked meal, to now—when I just want to feel like your little girl again!

❧

All of those times when you gave up something you wanted to do and opted for something I wanted to do.

❧

The thousands of times you said, "Shoulders back, chest out, stomach in..."

❧

Every Christmas and Easter you stayed up most of the night before to make sure the day would be absolutely perfect for us, as tired as it made you.

❧

The first time you told me I had a guardian angel.

❧

Mommy Magic
Adria Manary

When my helium balloon flew out of my hands and I said it was okay because Grandma would catch it in heaven...and you cried.

The fact that you have never broken a promise...except of course when you had to rush to the hospital to have my brother when you had promised to play cards with me!

Our many car trips and my famous lines that echo around the world... "Are we there yet? I have to go to the bathroom. Does the hotel have a pool?"

Always doing your very best to make my wishes come true...even to-day, if at all within your power!

The time you got a letter from the insurance company raising your insurance because of a speeding ticket I got on the way back to col-lege...the one I "forgot to tell you about."

The many colds you got because you came to every ice hockey prac-tice and game.

Family nights...bowling, Parcheesi, canasta, movies, Uno...

Meatloaf dinners on Thursdays.

The way you have always supported and loved Dad.

Being the team mom every time you could be.

Driving my friends and me all over the place!

The many prayers you have said silently on my behalf.

Letting me make my own mistakes.

The times (although few) you let me stay home from school even though I wasn't physically sick. I will always afford my children those "mental health" days, as you used to call them.

The discipline you instilled in me.

The way you could always get me to laugh when I was angry... and still can!

The nights you stayed up with me until the wee hours listening to every word I said with compassion and empathy.

Mommy Magic
Adria Manary

The fact that you have never lost the little girl inside you.

❦

The first time all of the neighbors came over on Christmas Eve and you played Christmas carols on the piano and everyone sang. I never knew you could even play the piano until that night!

❦

The way you never allowed me to say, "I can't."

❦

Mommy Magic
Adria Manary

A Widow's Request

Stories presented at the end of each chapter are by other mothers whose stories were chosen because they best exemplified the meaning of that chapter. However, the following is a story I wrote about another mom, who did something for her daughters I shall never forget, and illustrated the meaning of this chapter in a beautiful way. I did not mention her name in the original *Mommy Magic*, out of respect for what she had gone through, and because she is quite famous. In this edition, I shall reveal whom this story is about since she has gone through the healing process, and I would like to give her the credit she deserves.

I went to high school with Katie Couric, CBS anchor woman and former television show host of The Today Show on NBC. I had not talked with her in years, but a serious illness that both of our husbands were fighting at the same time brought us back together. We supported each other through parts of the ordeal, but Jay, the love of her life and the father of her two precious children, tragically lost the battle. I'll never forget what she whispered in my ear when I hugged her at the gravesite after his funeral. "Don't worry," she said, "Joel will be fine." Bless her soul, she was right; my husband won his "battle with the beast"...but that she would try to ease the worrisome thoughts she innately knew I was having, at the time when she needed and deserved my support was, to say the very least, amazingly selfless, and appreciated more than she will ever know.

It was what she did prior to that moment, however, that I would like to share in respect to this chapter. For Jay's funeral, the family received dozens and dozens of beautiful floral arrangements and their charity of choice was blessed with generous donations. Fortunately for Katie and her young children, there was an enormous amount of support from family and friends, and her celebrity status provided for much public support. In her infinite wisdom, however, she knew that soon people's lives would return to normal, and the support would naturally lessen. As much as she appreciated the outpouring of sympathy, she wanted something more for her precious children...something that would last. To accomplish this goal, she asked those close to her husband to write a story about him, as they knew him. They could be stories from his childhood, college days, marriage, fatherhood, career adventures— anything they were moved to write. These requests were made privately, but also at the funeral in a touching and heartfelt request. She planned to put a book together for their daughters about Daddy—full of the wonderful memories of those who also loved him. It would be a very special collection they could look back on as they themselves went off to college, met the men of their dreams and started their own families...all their dad would love to have been a part of in this world, but now would be watching from above. They may not be able to feel his touch over the years, but they will certainly feel the magic of his existence through this ardent tribute to their loving father.

Mommy Magic
Adria Manary

A Fresh Look

A child's heart overflows with joy
Their love is fresh and true.
Their eyes look clearly on the world
Few tears have blurred their view.

Childhood is a special place
Where trust and love abound—
The smallest things bring happiness
Like puppies, hugs and clowns.

Remember how you saw the world
When you were only three.
Then close your eyes and fill your mind
With thoughts that set you free.

Clear away your worries
And rest in solitude—
Then look into your child's bright face
With refreshed gratitude.

Children see with their hearts,

until they are taught to see only with their eyes.

— Anonymous

Mommy Magic
Adria Manary

The Whole World is Magic Through the Eyes of a Child

*T*ake time, at least once a day, to look at the world through the eyes of your child—rather than through your own. You'll be amazed at what you see. Often you will catch a glimpse of their childhood wonder, and sometimes you will see a particular situation differently—as viewed through their eyes. Part of the magic of being a mother is the bond you have with your child that lets you know how he's feeling or what she's thinking. The key is to make sure you act on what those feelings tell you. Your child will appreciate the occasions when you take the time to do so. Situations that seem unimportant to you, may hold high importance to your child.

Kids do say the darndest things, as Art Linkletter so beautifully pointed out to us on television and in his wonderfully humorous books—but sometimes what they say might be funny to you, yet serious to them. Mr. Linkletter tells of a six-year-old who, when told he had no school because it was George Washington's birthday, asked if he could go to George's party. How priceless! However, our response to a comment like that should not be laughter alone. We would need to explain why he can't go, as well as why we were laughing. To them, they're missing a party if they're not told there is no party—and they may even be hurt that we would laugh at them. Laughing with our children rather than at our children is extremely important...and the difference between the two is very slight. I have been amazed at how many times my sensitive little children have asked why I'm laughing at them when that wasn't what I meant at all!

When my oldest son was eight years old, my husband and I were hosting a large affair in an elegant room of the Congress building in Washington, D.C. Since it was just a few weeks before Christmas, we asked each attendee to bring a toy for underprivileged children. We asked two charities to send a representative to collect the toys, and decided it would be a golden opportunity for our son to experience the art and pleasure of giving. Therefore, we asked him to give a short speech and then present the toys to the charities. He wrote a wonderful little speech and sat patiently through the evening until his time came to speak and make the presentation.

One of the charities represented there was the Prison Fellowship Foundation. They were going to give the toys to the children of parents who, sadly, would be spending Christmas in prison. The other was an abused children's home. Of course I had read the speech my son had written and was pleased and proud. The last sentence of the speech, as he wrote it, went like this: "I feel bad for those kids whose parents are in jail and hope these toys will make them happy. I'm very happy my mom and dad take such good care of me and that they also thought of taking care of so many other kids this Christmas too."

The problem was that he did not read it as he had written it. Instead, his last sentence went like this: "And I'm so glad that I have parents who love me and I'm very happy that they're out of jail!"

"What did he say?!" I thought.

You can imagine the looks on both my husband's and my faces as 500 people looked at us and wondered when we were in jail...and why!!! I guess the shocked look on our faces cued the audience that we were innocent, and they broke out in a roar of laughter that my son was embarrassed about for years. The first time I retold the story, he cried and left the room. I had no idea until that moment he felt that way and it broke my heart. From then on I would tell it when he was not present. Not until he was thirteen, when we had a long talk about the difference between laughing at and laughing with, did he understand the audience was truly laughing at his comment rather than at him personally. After that he told the story himself and laughed. Great movies have been made where the parent and child switch places and end up understanding each other much better during the process. In the real world, however, all you can do is try to see things through the eyes of the child within you as much as possible. This chapter will give you ideas on how to see the world from one to four feet tall, and create an even closer bond between you and your munchkins!

Mommy Magic
Adria Manary

The voyage of discovery lies not in finding new landscapes, but in having new eyes.

— Marcel Proust

When your child wants to talk to you, get down on their level. Kneel down so you can look directly into their eyes, or have older ones sit on the couch with you.

When you say, "wait a minute," it seems like an hour to them... especially if it does turn into an hour. So, be as accurate as possible when you tell them how long it will be.

When you tell a lie, it teaches them to lie. Think about what is going through their little heads when you think you're telling an innocent lie to get out of doing something.

When they get an "A-"on their report card—don't ask why there's a minus—just be proud of the "A"!

Don't just watch them play all the time—join in often. Reading a book as they play at your feet brings far less joy than joining in. The challenge is not just to babysit and make sure they're safe—but to interact and make sure they know you deem them a fun playmate.

The Whole World is Magic...Through the Eyes of a Child

Call a local pizza parlor and ask for a tour. It's best if you go in a group. The children will find it fascinating, and the pizza will taste even better as they talk about the pizza man who "created" it! You won't look at pizza the same way ever again!

❦

Find ways to enjoy the things your children find pleasure in that you would otherwise avoid! I am still amazed at how much my little girl used to love roly-poly bugs. Her love of bugs in general and my intense dislike of them is the only difference I have found between us thus far. However...I learned to actually hold and examine many little creatures because I did not want to destroy her high value of them. And to tell you the truth...those roly-poly bugs are sort of cute!

❦

A child's imagination is often the best place they can go to have fun. If your child has an imaginary friend, set a place for the friend at the table. If he is fighting an alien, hand him a cookie sheet as a shield. Find as many ways as you can to enhance their imagination by becoming a part of it on a daily basis.

❦

A trip to the grocery store may be mundane to you, but to your child it can be an adventure. New people, so much to look at, and GOODIES! If your child is old enough, let him find things on the list and bring them back to put in the cart. For younger ones, let them pick one item you will buy for them while you're there. Have them look for the item as you venture down each aisle. In the meantime, let them help you with your list by asking who can see the next item first!

❦

Mommy Magic
Adria Manary

Remember—children learn the most through observation!
If you want them to be kind, show kindness.
If you want them to have good manners, be courteous.
If you want them to appreciate learning, let them see you reading
your own books.

&

What you DO...they will TOO...and their memories are phenomenal.
The following is one of my favorite illustrations:

A three-year-old "big" sister constantly supervised her mother when
she changed the newborn. After one rushed session, completed
without the typical sprinkling of powder, the child corrected Mom:
"Wait," she cried, "you forgot to salt him!"

&

Choose your battles wisely. Remember it's good for a child to feel
they can win once in awhile. As I watched my little boy writing in
the steam on the mirror after a hot bath, I really wanted to tell him
to stop because it would mess up the mirror, it wouldn't dry clear...
all of the things my mom used to tell me. But something in my mind
stopped the words from coming out of my mouth, and I was never
gladder. As he finished the heart and wrote, "I LOVE MOMMY,"
I decided I might never enforce that rule again!

&

Often we can learn from the eternal, innocent optimism of children,
as the following story illustrates:

When a mother saw a thunderstorm forming in mid-afternoon, she
worried about her seven-year-old daughter who would be walking
the three blocks from school to home.

Deciding to meet her, the mother saw her walking nonchalantly along, stopping to smile whenever lightning flashed.

Seeing her mother, the little girl ran to her, explaining happily, "All the way home God has been taking my picture!"

❧

Sit on the floor A LOT.

❧

Teach your children not just to look...but to truly see.

❧

Have you ever noticed how a child can get so angry at a friend, and yet make up so quickly and easily...like nothing ever happened? Try looking through the eyes of the child you used to be the next time someone upsets you. Letting go of anger quickly will offer you the innocent peace of a childlike heart, and will strengthen your child's value of forgiveness.

❧

Take a good look at yourself through your child's eyes.

❧

Mommy Magic
Adria Manary

In the interest of the theme of this chapter, two "special moment stories"
will be shared instead of one because Anne Gallant did not want either of her sons
to feel left out. She has so many loving tales she could tell about them both,
she wrote a story about each of them. As my mom used to say
to my brother and me—"Fair is fair!"

Peirson's View

—by Anne Rogers Gallant

I inherited many wonderful traits from my parents, but I never was quite thrilled about my head of tousled, curly hair. At its best it has always been out of control, and it is red. Throughout its existence, my long and unruly hair has been repeatedly wrangled into braids, arm-wrestled into ponytails, and generally confined to quarters by an array of barrettes, hairpins, and other assorted devices. The goal was to keep it out of my face, and away from the population at large.

This truce served me well as I danced, played, ran, and swam my way through childhood. I even took pride in the nicknames my mop generated—Cousin It, Veronica Lake, and even Medusa. I liked having a name for every hair personality, and I liked having a head with many personalities—depending on the humidity.

Through my imagination, I could be a movie star, or dance the "Nutcracker." My hair became an integral prop for these make-believe fantasies.

As the years passed, I spent an ever-increasing portion of my life trying to straighten, fix, change, and just plain deal with my rebellious red mane. The magical connection with my hair disappeared and eventually, my hair and I could not even keep our childhood truce.

One day, however, my youngest son, Peirson, who was four years old, came into my bathroom to visit while I was dressing...as was his custom. (Mothers throughout the world know the word "privacy" does not exist in our children's vocabularies!) I had just reached the "What shall I do with my hair today?" phase of the process.

As I furiously swept my hair down from its "circle" (what Peirson and his older brother Karl call my hair when it's wound up in a bun), I saw my precious little baby staring at me in the mirror with a quizzical look in his eyes.

He suddenly exclaimed, "MOMMY! Are you a MERMAID?"

I turned around and looked into his tiny, angelic face. He was gazing at my red, unruly hair with a look of excitement and awe. "You are SO beautiful!" he continued.

As I scooped him into my arms to thank him for such a wonderful compliment, he said, "You must be Ariel, Mommy!"

I gave him a big kiss, and as I glanced into the mirror, the view was—just for a second—a cascading bouquet of fiery locks. And for a moment, I saw what he saw...and it truly was magical.

My young son scampered away, but quickly returned clutching a fork in his little hand. He had remembered how mermaids comb their hair, and wanted to help.

Together, Peirson and I finished the job of, "What shall I do with my hair today?" For the first time in years, it didn't seem like a struggle at all.

Mommy Magic
Adria Manary

Mommy is Always with Me

—also by Anne Rogers Gallant

*I*n our family we always had something called a "there-there." Every family has one. It's that thing—a blanket, stuffed animal, bottle, whatever—that makes a baby (on up to an adult) feel better...just because.

Our oldest son, Karl, came home from the hospital wrapped in a sweet, soft, white receiving blanket with satin borders...his future "there-there." As he grew it stayed with him always. He HAD to have it. As we waited for all of those incredible firsts, I was delighted one day when out came a word that to me sounded very much like "Mommy." Much to my chagrin, it turned out to be "money." We weren't sure why or where it came from (although my late father had been a banker and we wondered if it was Daddy's heavenly joke to us). Whatever the origin, it soon became clear what "money" was—it was Karl's blanket, his "there-there." From that moment on we never really used the word blanket again. I would even wake up cold in the middle of the night and say to my husband, "Honey, you've got all the money!" It was one of our special family words.

When Karl was very young I never left him. When I finally decided it was time to branch out, he would work himself up into such a state that he would literally get sick at his stomach. It broke my heart, but I knew I had to help us both get past this obstacle. The first time I left him with a babysitter was miserable. I can still see that tiny, perfect face peeking out of his "money" with tears streaming down it. Choking back my own tears, I told him that Mommy would be back soon. Then I wrapped his money all cozy around him and said, "Mommy is always with you."

Over the next few years I watched with mixed and often selfish emotions, as his young world grew slowly but surely larger. At times, it seemed as if he couldn't wait to get away from the nest. As any mommy knows, this is both traumatic, as well as the reason why we exist.

The very first time our increasingly sophisticated, then seven-year-old went for an overnight, I went to his room to help him pack. I wanted to make sure something other than Legos, action figures, and Pokemon cards went into his suitcase. When I walked into his room he was furiously stuffing his "money" into his bag.

He looked up at me as if he had been caught with his hand in the cookie jar. "I'm taking my money with me. Do you think it's okay?"

"Of course, Darlin'! You can take anything you want," I replied.

Then he said words I will treasure forever, "It will be good to have it...cause it means Mommy is always with me." Once again, I choked back tears.

Well, he made it through the night, which is more than I can say for myself. I didn't sleep at all! There were many sleepovers after that and it got easier every time for him, but not for me. It all happened so quickly, but the one thing that never changed was that he always took his "money" (though slightly frayed and worn from all the love) with him.

Fast forwarding to the present, it's hard for me to believe that he is now away at college! But the wonderful assurance that was first symbolized in a blanket, is now firmly entrenched in our hearts...that even if only in spirit, mommy will always be with him!

Mommy Magic
Adria Manary

Childhood Magic

The enchanting world of childhood
Is in a mother's hands.
For there is a special magic,
That only she commands.

This magic is a special gift
That comes from God above…
Given when a child is born,
Then nurtured by her love.

Through wisdom and devotion
A mother guides her child.
Though laughter and enchantment
Are as important and worthwhile.

There are many happy moments
As our children go through life.
But when the disappointments come
This "magic" lessens strife.

Those warm and charming moments
Ingrained in childhood years
Are a comfort when those troubled times
Bring sadness, grief and tears.

But most of all the magic
Soothes the heart and soul
And cultivates the happiness
That is this life's true goal.

Magic is the study of intention.

Teach your children to trust their inner

guidance system—because they have the

"magic" right inside of themselves!

— Stephanie Yeh

3

Enhancing the Magic of Childhood Fantasies

*C*an you imagine growing up without having had a little magic to make the world a more enchanting place? Imagine the holidays that would never have been the same. Losing teeth would have just been painful...and the quarter your grandfather pulled out of your ear would have lost its luster.

What about the happiest place on earth—Disneyland? How could it exist without magic? Belief in the magic of life is the key to enjoying it. However you define magic—have fun with it. From the magic of love to the magic of the hummingbird, the world is what you make it.

As suggested earlier, we are responsible for "creating" the world as our children see it. Our outlook on life will most likely become their outlook. So utilizing the magic we possess to create magic in their lives is a gift that will last forever.

In this chapter we will explore magic that will let your child delight in the fantasies of childhood. Along with the traditional fantasies that come with the holidays, we will also offer ways to take advantage of the moment.

One such time occurred while our family was visiting Disney World, when my boys were ages three and five. After a long and quite magical day, I was presented with a marvelous opportunity as we sat on the curb of Main Street and watched Tinkerbell fly down from the castle—followed by an amazing display of fireworks. When we got up to leave, Chase and Dane spied those eye-catching wands that look as if they are sprinkling color into the air. Unfortunately they had seen them in the hands of other children, and the vendor selling them had closed for the evening. They were very sad, but too tired to whine for long. I told them that wishes often came true at this magical place, and maybe they should wish for the wands. They loved the idea and made the wish out loud to Mickey.

The next day I awakened before they did, and raced out to buy the two wands. I put them in a bag with a "note" from Mickey, and then placed them outside the door. The suite in which we were staying was two levels, so when they awakened I had my husband keep them upstairs so I could sneak downstairs to ring the doorbell, and run quietly back to the couch. I yelled for them to answer the door, which they did with great enthusiasm. "We don't know anybody here!" yelled one. "Who could it be?!" cried the other.

When they opened the door and looked in the bag, their eyes grew as big as saucers. "It's the wands we wished for! And there's a note!" Chase yelled as he ran over to me. "Read it, read it!"

"WOW," I said. "It's from Mickey Mouse!"

"What does it say, what does it say?" they screamed.

"It says, Wishes really DO come true at Disney World...Love, Mickey."

Fortunately I had remembered to supply the batteries so the wands illuminated immediately before their eyes.

"WOW," cried Chase. "WOW," copied Dane. They were happily entertained the rest of the morning, and repeated the story to everyone who would listen that day. It was a day all of us will remember forever.

Please let me caution you that this chapter is for parents' eyes only... we wouldn't want to give away any secrets!

Mommy Magic
Adria Manary

There are only two ways to live your life:
One is as though nothing is a miracle.
The other is as though everything is a miracle.

— Albert Einstein

As long as children are continually reminded that the real magic lies within them because God lives in their hearts, having some fun with enchanting tales will make their childhoods that much more memorable...

Sprinkle green glitter around on St. Patrick's Day and leave a special gold coin for each child. Those leprechauns can be mischievous, too!

Have a neighbor dress as Santa Claus and peek in the windows the week before Christmas. Have him ring sleigh bells outside to start the fun. I'll never forget my son yelling out of the sliding glass door as Santa slipped through our back gate, "Santa—I've been a real good boy!"

Before your child sits on Santa's lap, slip him a note letting him know what items your child will be getting for Christmas. Then Santa can say a definite yes to those particular presents and your child will be thrilled and more convinced at Christmas.

Enhancing the Magic of Childhood Fantasies

Never forget the importance of the Tooth Fairy and the Easter Bunny!

&

When a member of the family or a friend gets sick, after saying a prayer for them, hold your child's hand, and tell them they can send a magic thought to the person to make them feel better. Sending love can work miracles!

&

Learn a few simple magic tricks to amaze your children and their friends. You'll soon be the hit of the neighborhood!

&

Teach your children some magic tricks so they can amaze their friends.

&

My son went through a terrible period where he would have night-mares every night. After having tried everything, he spied a "dream catcher" in an Indian reservation store. He knew about them, be-cause a friend of his had one. "Oh, Mommy," he said, "maybe it will catch my bad dreams!" I immediately agreed and prayed it would work (the real magic!). To my delight, he hung it on his top bunk, and informed me the next week the bad dreams had stopped!

&

Always throw a penny in a fountain and make a wish! With little ones, have them share their wishes with you. Often you can make the wish come true, and what an impression that makes! I'll never forget a wish my daughter made. When I asked what she had wished for she simply said, "I wished that I'll be a good mommy when I grow up...just like you!"

&

Mommy Magic
Adria Manary

Add a dash of love to every meal you make. Touch your fingers to your heart and then act like you're sprinkling the love from your heart onto the food. Be sure to tell your children what the special ingredient is!

⚘

When we traveled across country with three young children, a dog and a ferret, we were looking for every way possible to make the trip more magical, memorable, and tolerable. Strictly by accident, I came up with the "magic window"—which kept my four-year-old entertained constantly throughout the trip. She asked if she could open the window one day, and I said, "Sure!" But instead of using the button, she started pointing at the window with her index finger, and pulling her finger down. Almost by instinct, I moved my finger to the driver's controls and made the window come down with her finger as she directed it to open. She was so surprised and thrilled she squealed, "Did you see that?!" "Oh yes!" I answered. "You must be magic!"

⚘

Pick a star that's viewable most of the time and name it after your child. If you want it to be official, go to www.starregistry.com and they will register a star in your child's name (for a price). Every evening you can see their star, make wishes on it—or talk about how incredibly special your child is—and how they always need to "reach for the stars!"

⚘

Have the Good Behavior Fairy visit your home on occasion. This fairy leaves treats for children who are especially well-behaved. It can be a balloon with a congratulatory note tied to the doorknob of their bedroom, so when they wake up they have a fun surprise.

Enhancing the Magic of Childhood Fantasies

Or it could be a small toy laid on their pillow, so they spy it when they pull down the covers to crawl into bed. Choose whatever your particular child would consider a reward.

Ask a friend to call or visit at an exact time. Then when the telephone or doorbell rings, pause for a moment and say, "That's _____." Your children will definitely think you're amazing. Of course, you'll probably have to arrange it a few times to convince older children!

Tell them your wish came true when they were born!

Write a secret message that has to be read in a mirror to "decode." Guess-who-loves-you is a fun one!

When you have to be away from your child, give them a piece of jewelry, or other special item to "talk" to you through, and show them what you'll be using as well. A necklace works well. If your child can tell time, it's good to set a time when you both will send messages of love to each other—or "I can't wait until you come home" messages. Of course they can do it anytime they would like as well.

My daughter was very upset one day as I was leaving (even though I was only going to be gone an hour!), so I looked down at her little heart necklace and said, "Did you know that your heart is magic?"

She stopped sniffling for a moment and said, "It is?" I had gotten her attention off the problem of my walking out the door!

Mommy Magic
Adria Manary

"The heart inside of you is magic, and so is the one on your necklace. It is a symbol of the love you have inside of you."

"Really?!"

"Yes," I said, eased by her hopeful eyes. "And if you want to talk to me, all you have to do is talk into that heart, and I will feel your love."

"Okay," she said, smiling. "Are you going to talk to me?"

"Of course," I said enthusiastically. "I will use my ring...all right?"

"ALL RIGHT," she said.

Then I hugged her, kissed her and handed her to Daddy. This time she waved and smiled.

Remember to teach your children the magic of thought. The age-old saying "you are what you think" holds much truth. The earlier your children learn this, the better they'll be at living it.

Dress up for Halloween, conjure up some surprises, and make your house the talk of the neighborhood kids...and yours!

Have your children create "giving" lists as well as wish lists.

Remember to give the gift of time during the holidays. It is a wonderful lesson for your children that "things" are not as important as spending time together and performing kindnesses for one another.

The post office keeps letters to Santa for people who might want to answer the ones from people in need. Be the Claus family, and buy some of the things on the lists and deliver them to a needy family. The smiles on their faces will be the best gift you and your family receive all season.

Have the Tooth Fairy, Santa, and the Easter Bunny leave little notes with the goodies. It makes them seem much more real!

As a birthday, Christmas, Chanukah, or any other holiday present, give your child a year full of treats by making a coupon booklet listing one treat they will receive each month. This way the gift will last all year (and the expense can be drawn out over twelve months).

When your child's feelings are hurt, pretend you have a magic wand and wave it over their head—and then their heart—saying you are pulling out their heartache and pouring the love back in.

Don't forget to accentuate the magic of love as the greatest magic of all!

Brianna's Magical Land

−byLorena Serna

*I*n my life I have had the wonderful opportunity to travel abroad extensively, meet interesting people, and take part in the diverse cultures these countries had to offer. However, these experiences pale in comparison to the majestic world my daughter, Brianna, has shown me—a world I knew as a child, but had forgotten. I consider myself blessed to be given the chance to visit this world again with my daughter as my guide. Throughout our travels together we have seen fire-breathing dragons that are kind at heart, fairies with irides-cent wings shimmering with all the colors of a rainbow, and prin-cesses who fall in love and live happily ever after.

Recently, I took my daughter on a picnic to a nearby wooded park. While lying on the blanket, we saw clouds transform themselves into ponies and puppies. We lowered our heads to where the grass around us became as tall as city skyscrapers and dragonflies soared above like helicopters. A bee buzzing around was no longer just pollinating the flowers, but was telling them stories of his adventures in valleys far away. Two squirrels were playing a game of chase in the treetops overhead, and Brianna informed me they should be careful because the trees were so tall and they might fall and hurt themselves. Regarding this matter, I sincerely expressed my agreement.

After we had eaten our lunch, we went for a walk in the woods. With Brianna leading the way, I soon learned Indians made the path we traveled on—a fact she pointed out after finding a feather that surely must have fallen from the headpiece of a great chief. Once we reached the lake, we were greeted by jabbering geese who were arguing amongst themselves as to which one of them would be first to eat the breadcrumbs from Brianna's hand. She made sure they all received equal portions, including the smallest one who had missed out on a few because he did not move as fast as the others. On our way back through the woods, Brianna found a wizard's staff. She pointed out how this was a very rare find, because it looked just like a stick and was often overlooked by those who could not tell the difference. She picked it up and proceeded to show me the proper way to hold it in order to get the most use out of its magic. While she held it in her right hand, she pressed the end on the ground. She informed me she had seen wizards do this to give themselves strength while on their long journeys.

A short time later, a small butterfly fluttered up to my daughter—who, by the way, is fluent in the language of butterflies. It informed her it was lost and afraid. As she held the butterfly on her finger and brought it close to her face, she told it she would help it find its way home. Amazingly, it sat quietly on her finger for the remainder of the trek. Brianna continued to reassure it that it was now safe and did not need to be afraid. When we reached the clearing at the edge of the woods, Brianna lifted her hand and the butterfly flew away. She then turned towards me and let me know that the butterfly had told her it recognized the meadow and knew its way home.

As I watched her waving goodbye to the butterfly, the child inside me understood—and the mother I had become rejoiced in the moment.

These times are precious and I want to grasp onto all of them and hold them close. I know she will have many more adventures throughout her life, and all of her journeys will have a special magic. I am just grateful that, for the moment, she is sharing her magical world with me.

Mommy Magic
Adria Manary

The Mommy Magnet

I awakened this morning early
With a foot attached to my leg
As I tried to gently separate
Her little voice said, "Let's play!"

Then I sat up in the bed
As her hand slipped into mine
I smiled and squeezed her fingers
For we are always intertwined.

I stood up, stretched and felt her eyes
Looking into mine
Her arms outstretched—that "carry me" look
I lifted her and sighed.

We nestled in each other's arms
As we enjoyed our bottle and coffee
And then I felt my feet get warmed
By our adoring little puppy.

Suddenly I heard a cry
My six-year-old awakened
Down the stairs he ran to me
Still a little shaken.

He climbed across the dog
And up onto my lap
Blanketed with love
There was only one spot left.

I heard another door and spied
Another smiling face
My oldest walked in sleepily
And calmly took his place.

My husband came to say goodbye
And gave us each a kiss
He knew he left us happy
Together in our bliss.

The phone can ring, the chores can mount
My work can loudly beckon.
But nothing's more important
Than cuddling my sweet children.

It's as if I am a magnet—
A power truly treasured.
For the closeness that I share with them—
One could never measure.

Mommy Magic
Adria Manary

Tender Moments

I often tell my children they'll always be my babies. Then, I proceed to tell them how their dad's mother still calls him her baby, so they will be my babies for a long, long time to come! However, it's hard to keep your little boy a baby once he starts playing ice hockey—and can run faster than you. Suddenly you feel like maybe you ought to honor his journey into manhood and stop some of those babying ways. It's tough to think about, but a mom's gotta do what a mom's gotta do, right? Well—almost. Take heart, moms. The following story is one of my fondest memories, and will renew your hope in keeping them your babies for a little while longer.

One night as I was tucking my ten-year-old into bed, he said, "Mom, will you sing me a song?"

Taken aback that he would ask, since he had sort of ducked my kiss at school that day, I said, "Of course, honey. What made you think of that?" I couldn't help but ask since it had been a few years since I had sung him to sleep.

He said, "I was trying to get Astra (his little sister) to sleep last night and she asked me to sing a song to her. I asked her why, and she told me that was how you helped her to go to sleep."

"Do you remember me singing to you?" I asked.

"Sort of...but I'd like to hear you do it again," he said softly.

"I would love to, sweetheart." I began to the tune of "Lullaby and Goodnight." "My little boy...is such a joy...and I l-o-v-e him dearly..." I continued to make up words as I went, and he seemed to put every word into his little heart.

At the end he said, "That is so cool. Did you actually make that up as you went?" I said that was how I always sang to them—telling them how I felt in my heart, and assuring them of my love as their mom and also of God's great love for them. He was truly happy as he drifted off to dreamland.

A few weeks later, he came in while I was rocking my Astra to sleep, again singing to her. He stayed and listened for a few minutes and then disappeared. After I had laid her down he came into my room and asked me if I would rock him to sleep too. My heart filled with so much "mommy joy" that of course I leapt at the chance.

I carried him into his room, where his little brother sat on the floor struggling to get his shoes off. I couldn't help but think the moment would be lost, but I calmly turned off the light, and sat with him in a chair. Even with his brother as a potential teasing witness, he asked if I could hold him like I had Astra. So I did...and once again, I made up a song just for him. I rocked back and forth—singing and looking into his face until his eyes started closing. His brother just sat silently, watching and listening.

As I struggled to get him into the top bunk, he again told me how cool it was. But this time, it wasn't only the song. He said, "Mom, you know how you say your love is like a blanket that covers us and makes us feel warm and safe?"

"Yes," I answered, with my eyes filling up quickly.

"Well, it was weird, because that's exactly how you made me feel when you were rocking me. It was like I was dreaming and I didn't want to move." He went on and on, and all I could think was he was actually feeling the magic of the warmth and love I felt for him. It was a mommy moment I shall never forget. As I kissed him goodnight, I said, "Well, we'll just have to do that more often." He nodded happily and closed his eyes. And yes, I rocked his brother to sleep that night too. It was indeed a magical evening.

Tender moments are a natural part of mothering and most often come spontaneously. The suggestions in this chapter will offer ways to enhance the closeness that is cherished by every parent and child.

Tender moments...

One by one,

shine in the heart

As bright as the sun.

– Adria Manary

Mommy Magic
Adria Manary

The best and most beautiful things in the world cannot be seen or even touched.

They must be felt with the heart.

—Helen Keller

When your child does something that reminds you of yourself when you were little, take time and share a story from your childhood with them. They love to picture their parents as kids!

Hold hands with your child out of love often—not just when you're crossing the street.

Tell your children that your day just isn't right until they give you "morning hugs!"

Family hugs are also important. Get the whole family together and stand in a big circle and hug each other...often.

Tickling your children to sleep or stroking their hair as they drift off to dreamland is just as important as reading to them before bed.

If your child still uses a bottle, enjoy a "ba-ba and coffee" as you snuggle together in the morning. The warmth will come from the heart as well as your coffee mug. For older children, pour them a hot cup of milk with a bit of honey in it or a mug of hot chocolate.

&

Gather everyone under the covers with a flashlight, and read a story that touches the heart.

&

Sometimes the way we kiss our children when they're off to an activity or school is like the famous Hollywood kiss on each cheek and "let's do lunch" attitude. Once in a while when you hug your child, tell them that you can't let go...and make it a very long hug!

&

Use sign language for a secret "I Love You" sign, and use it often with each other. Put your thumb, index finger and pinky up, bend the other fingers down, and touch the same fingers on your child as you look deeply into their eyes.

&

Sing special songs to your children with their names and your feelings for them. I use the tunes to well-known songs and change the words. For example, I sing "Lullaby and Goodnight" with these words:

> My precious girl
> With little curls
> She's so special to me...
> I love her through and through
> And she loves me too.

Mommy Magic
Adria Manary

I'm proud of her
My sweet daughter
She is thoughtful and kind,
And I thank God every day
That He sent her to be mine!

❧

When the moon is full, take a long evening walk with one of your children (take turns for one-on-one time). At whatever level that is age-appropriate, talk about the meaning of the first walk on the moon, and what the astronaut meant when he said, "One small step for man. One giant leap for mankind."

❧

Lay side by side on your big bed and hug each other close. Then roll with each other from one side of the bed to the other—sort of like a double cartwheel. You can hold your weight off of your little one with your elbows as you roll. My daughter and I did this once sort of by accident and then it became one of our favorite things to do. It creates lots of cuddly laughter!

❧

Continue to brush your child's hair—after the tangles are out. Then run your fingers through their hair and massage their scalp gently.

❧

You don't have to be near your child to share a tender moment with them. If you have to be away, call them and tell them you are hugging the phone and ask them if they feel it. One night my daughter was "talking" to her daddy on the phone. She hugged the phone to her heart rather than putting it to her ear. When she finally did put the phone to her ear, I could tell her dad had asked her why she had

Tender Moments

been so quiet. She said, "Daddy—didn't you feel it? I was hugging the phone since I know you're in there somewhere!" Then it was her father who was silent. "Daddy? Are you there?"

❧

Lie down with your child until he falls asleep. Bedtime does not have to be a battle if you take the time to soothe your children, making them feel secure and loved. Reading to them is wonderful, but being there as they drift off to dreamland is extra special. You are a much better security blanket than a piece of cloth!

❧

Look deeply into your child's eyes...for at least ten seconds. Tell them that you can see right down into their heart, and you like what you see!

❧

Rock your older child to sleep.

❧

Extend your "Mommy Magic" to families who might need a little extra love. There was a little girl in our old neighborhood whom I gave a hug to every day I saw her...which was almost every day. As soon as she would see me, she would start running to me and say: "Mrs. Manary, you haven't had your hug from me today!" I don't really know who was helping who—but it was something my own children came to understand the importance of.

❧

I have heard, and believe, the old saying: "The best thing a father can do for his children is to love their mother." Just remember, the reverse is also true. Let your children know how much you love their dad!

❧

Mommy Magic
Adria Manary

Learn the art of giving your baby a massage.

❦

Create a box full of hearts during February. Make twenty-eight red paper hearts, (or twenty-nine during those special leap years) and help your children think of ways they can show their love to others. Then list one idea on each heart and put them in the box. The idea is to pull one out each day and perform the act of love.

❦

Bathe with your baby sometimes. You can hold your little one easier, and it's much more fun...for both of you! Then use a great big towel you can both fit in. The closeness is heavenly!

❦

Instead of putting cold lotion on after a bath, put the bottle of lotion into the tub while your child is bathing. Then afterwards cover the baby with the nice warmth of the lotion and a big fluffy towel.

❦

Put clothes right from the dryer onto your children when they come out of a bath or in from a snowy day of fun.

❦

Take your child to the beach in the evening and sit quietly—listening only to the crashing surf.

❦

Remember butterfly kisses and Eskimo kisses and create your own special kinds of kisses. My daughter and I made up "cheek rubs," and my sons have developed their own special handshakes.

❦

Buy a comfy "snuggly" with wide straps...the kind that holds your baby in a little pouch, close to your body. Some of my favorite memories are having had each of my children next to my heart even when I needed my hands free to do something else. In some cultures, a baby is never without body contact because touch is considered to be so important to an infant. When a mother has to put her child down, another woman puts the "pouch" on.

Teach your baby sign language. Babies can learn this before they can talk and it will reduce their frustrations because they will be better able to communicate their needs. It will also create a special kind of bond between you and your baby.

Mommy Magic
Adria Manary

*O*ur daughter Ariana moved from baby to toddler with her share of the usual bumps and scraped knees. On these occasions, I'd hold out my arms and say, "Come see me." She'd crawl into my lap, we'd cuddle, and I'd say, "Are you my girl?" Between tears she'd nod her head yes. Then I'd say, "My sweetie, beetie Ariana girl?" She'd nod her head, this time with a smile. Then I'd end with, "And I love you forever, for always, and no matter what!" With a giggle and a hug, she was off and ready for her next challenge.

Ariana is now four and a half. We've continued "come see me" time for scraped knees and bruised feelings, for "good mornings" and "good nights."

A few weeks ago, I had "one of those days." I was tired, cranky and overextended taking care of a four-year-old, twin teenage boys and a home business. Each phone call or knock at the door brought another full day's worth of work that needed to be done immediately!

I reached my breaking point in the afternoon and went into my room for a good cry.

Ariana soon came to my side and said, "Come see me." She curled up beside me, put her sweet little hands on my damp cheeks, and said, "Are you my mommy?" Between my tears I nodded my head yes. "My sweetie, beetie mommy?" I nodded my head and smiled. "And I love you forever, for always, and no matter what!" A giggle, a big hug, and I was off and ready for my own next challenge.

Mommy Magic
Adria Manary

Have Some Fun Today

When we are blessed with a little one,
Life is filled with a new kind of fun.
The joy of childhood reappears
As we remember our younger years.

And as we amuse our new generation,
We again feel that awesome sensation
Of deep belly laughs and warm summer rains…
And realizing life, is simply a game.

A game to be played with the greatest of zest
And when it comes to playing, our children know best!
So let down the barriers that life can create
And have fun with your kids, before it's too late!

The Manary "fam" has always made FUN a priorty—whether we're rolling down the road or rolling down the river.

Mommy Magic
Adria Manary

The Magic of Having Fun

It is a child's duty to have fun—and a parent's challenge to provide as much of it as possible! The fun you afford your child is part of the magical world you are continually creating for them. Of course they need to learn responsibility, but that too can be presented in a positive and fun manner. Life, in itself, is magical when you really think about it. And the more of it you experience, the more magical it will seem!

Children are prone to laugh and have fun; it is their natural state of mind. I love it when my little girl starts laughing—just because her brothers start laughing—when she has no idea what they're even laughing at! Children do not have to plan fun like we do as adults...scheduling tee-off times, spending three weeks planning for a one-week vacation, buying the right clothes to play tennis. Of course, we need to provide fun activities for them at times, which is why I wrote this chapter. But if we follow their lead and try our best to make everything fun—then we're bound to have more of it than we could ever have planned!

The first book I ever wrote was entitled, *If It's Not Fun...Forget It*. Although it has yet to be published, I learned a great deal about how important this elixir of life truly is. Since having fun, playing, or just plain being silly usually leads to laughter, I also researched the benefits of this uniquely human capability. I interviewed people of all ages and celebrities like Robin Leach (host of the old TV show, Lifestyles of the Rich and Famous—who believe me, really knew how to have fun!), Phyllis Diller, Whoopi Goldberg, Liberace—even a member of the famous Rockettes. But the most interesting piece of information I came across was about Norman Cousins' experience with, and belief in, laughter. He was completely convinced laughter therapy had played a very significant role in saving his life! Thomas Carlyle, a Scottish writer born in the eighteenth century once said, "No man who has once heartily and wholly laughed can be altogether irreclaimably bad."

Emotionally, the benefits are obvious. But physically, it has only recently become common knowledge that laughing releases a chemical in your body that boosts your immune system. So having fun—just playing with your children—has an added benefit for parents as well as kids. According to several research studies, playing relieves stress, promotes flexibility, and helps to prevent and heal disease.

Have you ever thought about the word "disease?" If you break it down, it reads, "dis–ease"...meaning, "not at ease!" So, the more "at ease" you become, the less chance you will have of contracting a "disease"—which will give you a longer amount of time to enjoy your children and for them to enjoy you!

In this chapter I will simply list lots and lots of ways to have more fun! Sometimes we do not provide as many fun options as we'd like to because it's too hard to prepare them or think of one at the moment. Therefore I hope this list will make life a little easier for you in the planning department. Have fun!

It's kind of fun to do the impossible.

— Walt Disney

Serve breakfast in the bathtub when you're running late in the morning. A quick cinnamon toast waffle and a banana make a great finger food breakfast! Your children will be clean, full and happy when they get out!

Always have a dress-up box—for girls and boys—and have plenty of costume materials for visiting friends! I learned this a little late. My little boy went over to a friend's house when he was five and came home raving about the superhero outfits and animal masks he had played with. Since he had so much fun with the one I made up for him, I wish I'd thought of it when he was three. Oh well, his brother benefited earlier in his life!

Make everything talk. Of course the dolls and stuffed animals should have special voices, but other things can come to life as well. How about talking fingers or talking spoons—or better yet, talking food. When you're trying to get your child to eat some salad, you can have it say, "Oh please let me get into your tummy with the rest of my friends, Mr. Chicken Nugget and Mrs. French Fry. I know they miss me and I want to be with them! Don't you like being with your friends?"

Special dates with Mommy and Daddy (separately) are important. One-on-one time is special, fun, and often productive in finding out what's going on in their little minds.

Crazy rule-bending that doesn't hurt a thing is important in making your child understand that life is flexible. Eating the cake right out of the pan on their birthday (a family event. . . you can bake another for their birthday party) or starting a french fry fight (no mess, but all the fun of a real food fight) can surprise your child to no end and cause instant fun and laughter.

Teach your telephone number by singing it to the tune of "Twinkle Twinkle Little Star." Count the syllables—there are exactly seven...just like every phone number!

Hide their gifts on their birthdays, and write poems and clues as to where the presents are.

Let one day a month be each child's special day—where they get to choose the family activities (within reason), as well as sit in the front seat (unless you have air bags), watch their favorite shows, eat their favorite dinner and choose their own dessert.

Have a birthday party for your pet.

Mommy Magic
Adria Manary

Host a tea party for your little girl's stuffed animals. Then host one for her friends—for no special occasion.

⚭

Create a family history scrapbook for the past year. Let your child draw pictures and add keepsakes such as ticket stubs. This can be an ongoing project that can fill in when boredom strikes! Take it out and read it together on New Year's Eve.

⚭

Make up a special family holiday. Use your last name and add something fun like "Sensational Smiths Day." Use old white t-shirts and put the name on a shirt for each family member. Have a game where you commemorate the special aspects of your family. (For instance have each family member finish the following sentence: "The Smiths are sensational because...) Eat at your family's favorite restaurant. Do whatever your family likes to do best!

⚭

When doing chores, make a game out of it by using a timer. They have to be done by the time the last grain of sand drops to the bottom of the hourglass!

⚭

Schedule family nights.

⚭

Have a different family member be responsible for the prayers each night, and tell what they are thankful for.

⚭

Have the children write an adventure story about the family and ask the little ones to do the illustrations. The Mystery of the Lost Jones Diamond is one example where the family made up a story about their mom's engagement ring!

⟡

Switch places for a while—include the pets for real confusion! Your daughter can be the mom, her brother can be her, and you can be the parrot (after all, you're used to repeating everything, right?).

⟡

Encourage long-distance pen pals for your children—by e-mail or snail mail. Write to the mothers of potential pals to get the ball rolling if they are too young or too embarrassed to do it themselves.

⟡

Choose a philanthropic endeavor the family can do together. Sponsor a child through World Vision, Save the Children or another credible organization and have your child send pictures and letters each month with your sponsorship money. Or go to a homeless shelter for mothers and children and help serve meals. Or go to a nursing home and talk to the residents. They adore children.

⟡

Have a discussion about when they will be mommies and daddies. How many children are they going to have? Are they going to have boys or girls or both? What games are they going to play with them? How are they going to teach them right from wrong? Where are they going to live? You'd be surprised what comes out of this conversation. I know I was!

⟡

Mommy Magic
Adria Manary

Children love to get wet—it's THAT simple! My daughter used to play for an hour in the sink and not get bored. Water, plastic cups, and spoons do the trick. Add a doll and you've added another half hour to playtime. My older boys could play in the hot tub all afternoon. (I made the water warm rather than hot.)

Seek out the kind of bubble liquid that is edible. I had been a mom for over ten years, and I'd never seen it until my kids discovered this yummy and fun liquid at a Cracker Barrel restaurant. They just had to get some...and I obliged, thinking it was a pretty cool idea myself and couldn't wait to taste it! Needless to say—it was a big hit! When we got home, they took turns blowing bubbles off of the deck while others tried to catch them in their mouths below. Deck or no deck, one child or ten, it is a great activity, and a perfect "video moment." A bonus is that there is no soap that sometimes gets in the eyes and puts a damper on normal bubble activity.

Try bubble painting! Pour regular bubble liquid into small containers, add several drops of food coloring to each, stir, and the "paint" is ready! Give each child several pieces of paper (for lots of wonderful creations) and a little bubble wand. Then the fun begins! Have them dip their wands into their favorite colors and blow the bubbles directly onto the paper. Voila! Beautiful abstract prints and happy little artists! You might want to do this one outside, or cover an indoor area with an old sheet or drop cloth. (Remember the bubbles might get away!)

Put small tubs of water on a table, on the floor, or on the ground. Put waterproof dolls or action figures in the water with other toys the children can choose. This is a good time to explain what is waterproof and what can be damaged by water—and remember to cover what you don't want water on! After that, they'll be busy for a good while and water is easy to clean off of them and the area around them!

Arm everyone with squirt guns and join in on the fun as the moving target.

Give baths in the baby pool! Just fill it up with water as usual and squirt some Baby Bath solution into the water to make bubbles. Then let them play for as long as they want. When they get out, they're shiny clean! Fun for them, and less hassle for you to get them into the bathtub!

For some real water magic, put pepper in a glass of water and explain that each tiny piece represents a person swimming in the ocean. Then, tell them to watch what the people do when a shark's fin pops up in the middle. As you say this, put a drop of oil on top of the water and watch the "pepper people" scatter! (Okay enough with water. I'm feeling waterlogged...)

Put your favorite slow song on, pick your child up and slow dance with them.

Mommy Magic
Adria Manary

Have fun with their food. Make shapes and characters out of sandwiches, pancakes, or cookies. It makes lunchtime a lot more fun!

※

Teach your children to laugh at themselves. It is a very important quality that will give them peace and a better sense of humor as they grow up.

※

As we all know, spills and messes come with children. Instead of cleaning them up in disgust, try to lighten up once in awhile. It helps if you prepare for the likelihood of certain spills as well. For instance, let your child take their shirt off when eating chocolate ice cream. Then when they spill it on their tummy say, "Mmmmm, chocolate tummy!" And "eat up" their tummy!

※

Go to the pet store and play with the puppies, talk to the parrots, and wonder at the snakes.

※

Do something constructive as a family. It generates cooperation and teamwork, which are both essential elements of a happy home.
- Build a fort
- Create a videotape to send to relatives
- Paint a room that needs it
- Cook a special meal, with each person responsible for a certain part of it
- Make up a "continuing story" where the first person makes up a sentence, then each person that follows adds his own sentence to create the story. Make sure to record it for future listening fun!

※

The Magic of Having Fun

Go to the airport and watch the planes taking off. Have your children pretend they're on one of them. Where are they going?

Build a fire and roast marshmallows.

Have a Christmas-in-July party.

Have four children hold a big beach blanket and shake it like a parachute. Then add a stuffed animal. See how long they can keep it up in the air.

I like to call this game "The Clean Socks Challenge," with the hope that everyone will start out with clean feet and clean socks! Split the family into two teams (changing up sides to even them out as necessary). Then put a big blanket on the carpet, get down on all fours, and go for the socks! The object of the game is to pull the socks off the other team's feet. The first team with all bare feet loses! When I heard about this one, I couldn't wait to get home and play it with the whole family! Of course, knowing how my boys like to wrestle, and how things can escalate, be very careful and establish these rules: The only thing you can touch is the other person's feet (no holding on to their legs either!), everyone must stay on the blanket, no standing, and no sharp corners of furniture around!

Have a sponge relay. Divide the participating children into teams and line them up. The first child in each line is the leader. Each team will need two different-sized buckets and one sponge. (It helps if each team has their own color of buckets and sponge.) Set the larger bucket at the start line, filled with water. The second set of buckets should be smaller and are set at the finish line, empty. Each child will in turn take the sponge from the start bucket, run to the finish bucket, squeeze it into that bucket, and run back. The child gives the sponge to the next child in line and returns to the end of their line. The next child dips the sponge into the start water bucket and repeats. The first team to fill their bucket with water wins! Children may have many turns in order to fill the buckets up.

&

One thing is for sure...hearts come together when laughter abounds!

&

Just remember...being flexible allows for many more opportunities to have fun!

&

People are just about as happy

as they make up their minds to be.

— Abraham Lincoln

Fixing Things Can Be Fun!

—by Chris Sumstine

J grew up in a much simpler time—when watching fireflies in a jar could hold my attention for hours, the first snowfall of winter filled my heart with joy, and the sound of the ice cream man led to a resounding "Mom, we need money!" The words, "I'm bored" never escaped our lips.

I often tortured my three sons with the inconceivable notion that my younger brother and I "could play for six hours with two army men and never get bored." A look of horror would spread across their faces—"What? No buttons, no electronic sounds, nothing to plug in? What kind of fun could this be?" It is sad that many of today's children miss out on things like a Kool-Aid stand in the summer or a neighborhood snowball fight in the winter. I fondly remember setting out one day to prove to my oldest son that it was possible to have fun without buttons, power cords, and memory cards.

When my oldest son, Brian, was about five, he loved to pretend he was a "fix-it man." Recognizing an opportunity, I decided to let him become our family handyman. I created a crude tool belt out of an old apron and then sent Brian up to his room to find "tools" in his toy box. In no time, the belt was full of abandoned treasures now finding a new purpose. While my little boy gathered his tools, I went to the kitchen "junk drawer" and pulled out an old receipt book he could use to conduct his official "business." The adventure began! I took his hand and we walked to the front door. Although he was a bit unsure of what would happen next, his sense of adventure led him courageously. I shut the door. After waiting a few seconds the doorbell rang. I opened it to my adorable Mr. Fix-It Man. His cap was tipped precariously to the side and his new tool belt was secure around his waist. He was ready for duty! I told him how happy I was to see him since we had so many things around the house that needed fixing. For the next few hours, my son and I went happily from room to room "fixing things." He fixed pretend leaky pipes, toilets, sinks and sprinkler heads. He crawled along the floor on his belly and used his flashlight and fixed my broken washer and dryer, dishwasher, and refrigerator. Magically, now I had an oven that worked perfectly and a shower that didn't leak! After each item was "fixed," my son would proudly report, "That's all fixed up now ma'am!" Then he would write a receipt and present it to me for payment.

Each of us had a role to play, and neither stepped out of character the entire time the adventure played out. I was the happy, satisfied customer and he was "the boss," as he liked to call himself. When the adventure ended, Brian asked me if we could play "Mr. Fix-It Man" again, to which I happily replied, "Of course! You never know what will need fixing around here next." I'm happy to report my home was not in as much of a state of disrepair as it sounds. In fact, none of those things needed to be fixed at all, but to a five-year-old who let his imagination run wild, the place was a dump and he was just the guy to make everything right again!

After a long day "on the job," my little handyman was ready for a nap. As he slept, I quietly thanked God for the precious opportunity to show my little boy that the simplest joys in life are found in the most unexpected ways. No bells or whistles, no beeps or blips, no remote controls or joysticks...just the pure and simple pleasure of letting your imagination run free. I'll always remember this day fondly. No matter how old our children are or how much distance grows between us as they move from childhood into adulthood, these memories bind us together for life.

Crayons Come from Rainbows

The wonder of nature
Is truly astounding
From the tiniest seed
To flowers abounding.

A child finds great pleasure
In God's mighty works
Wherever they turn
His magnificence lurks.

"Did God make my crayons?"
My little one asked
"No, crayons come from rainbows."
In that thought he basked.

"I like the way He makes the clouds
And then puts pictures in them…"
I laughed inside and hugged him close—
His thoughts were oft such gems.

If a child is to keep alive his inborn sense of wonder, he needs the companionship of at least one adult who can share it... rediscovering with him the joy, excitement and mystery of the world we live in.

– Rachel Carson

Mommy Magic
Adria Manary

Magical Wonders of Nature

A mother's magic comes with much responsibility, part of which is to ensure that her children are continually aware of the many other wonders of the world. A mere walk can turn into an enchanting adventure, if you simply take the time to point out the many tiny creations God has placed here. Miracles happen every day—and children love to hear about them.

I once read a story written by a woman whose favorite memories of her mom were their daily trips to the mailbox. Why would a routine chore become such a treasured memory? It was because her mother made those walks extraordinary with little stories about all of the little creatures on the way there and back. Think about it. The baby ant who became a hero. The caterpillar who turned into a butterfly. The fertile ground they're walking on that will, or already has, produced pretty flowers or summer vegetables. And what if those stories included your child helping those little creatures? It's really easy if you let the child in yourself out for a while and let her imagination flow free. After awhile, let your child make up stories too. Then, you can combine your stories by taking turns making up every other sentence of the story.

Let's take that idea a step further. What if there was often something in the mailbox for them to look forward to? Arrange for mail to come to your child at least once a week. There are many "freebies" for kids. Or maybe a relative could send things. . .or mom could make up imaginary pen pals and tickle the computer herself if others can't! Then the trips would be filled with anticipation as well.

If it's a long walk in the country, great! If the mail comes to your door, make up another reason for a daily walk. Regardless of your own particular situation, you can always make your daily routine more fun by expressing interest in the nature around you. Walking the dog is another great reason to explore. Imagine how many friends he must make each day!

This chapter is full of ideas that will help you and your adored ones see the world as the truly magical place it is. Just like when your children made Santa come alive again, you will be delighted at how they will breathe life into the world around you.

> *A person who cares about the earth*
> *will resonate with its purity.*

—Sally Fox

Help your child find a special nature spot to think, write in a journal, read, draw, or just make pictures in the dirt. Make it special by marking it somehow. If your child is small, pick a spot nearby for yourself, so your little one is not too secluded. During the winter, choose a spot by a window where you can look out upon nature together if it's too cold. Point out how different the sky looks each day. How the trees change. How each snowflake is different.

Look at the leaves of a tree and find one with a bite out of it. Who ate it? Explain how a leaf is like a french fry to a beetle!

Go strawberry picking and let your children eat as many as they can without getting a tummy ache.

Add an orange grove to your list of places to go on vacation (right below Disneyland or Disney World) when visiting California or Florida.

Swim with the dolphins! Sea World has a dolphin interaction program for children six and over, as well as adults. It is an amazing experience and something they (and you) will never forget!

Magical Wonders of Nature

Catch lightning bugs and fill up a jar to make a lantern for a while.

⟡

Check out a book at the library that identifies bugs, trees, and other living things, and see how many your children can identify in your yard.

⟡

Spray paint on the snow. Just fill some spray bottles up with water and add a few drops of food coloring and voila! Snow paint! The kids can write their names, decorate the front yard, and "dress" their snow people...whatever they want!

⟡

A treasure hunt is always fun. Remember "X" marks the spot! Draw a map for them to follow in the yard or in the neighborhood with hints along the way and a "treasure" at the end. A twist on this idea is to let older kids make the map for the younger ones. It's just as much fun for them to use their imaginations creating it as it is following it!

⟡

Make sure rainy days are as happy as sunny days. When it rains, start the day out by saying, "Yeah, it's raining! We get to stay cozy all day!" And then sing this variation of "Rain, Rain, Go Away":

Rain, rain, stay here today.
The plants and trees are yelling HOORAY!
We can play inside for awhile,
So you can make nature wear a smile!

⟡

Parks are key! Utilize their programs and playgrounds regularly. In addition, make your children aware of the importance of keeping them pretty.

⚬

Sit quietly in the backyard and listen to nature sing to you and your children. Anyone who talks cannot stay for the concert.

⚬

Take advantage of your surroundings. If you live on the coast, go whale watching on the ocean and go to the beach for sunsets (or sunrises, depending which coast you're on). If you live by a lake, draw attention to the sparkles dancing on it at certain times of the day. If you live by a river—go fishing often! If you live in the mountains, go hiking. This idea may sound like common sense, but I lived in Washington, D.C. almost all of my life and never visited the White House!

⚬

Help the birds—and entertain your children—by putting out any kind of bird feeder. An easy one to make is to spread peanut butter on a pinecone and roll it in birdseed. Attach a string to it and hang it outside your window for instant entertainment. If you live in an area where hummingbirds are common, plant flowers that attract them. They are amazing creatures to watch. Be sure to explain to your children it is "scientifically impossible" for a hummingbird to fly! Now there's some magic!

⚬

Plant some grass seed in a cup and watch it grow. It's easy, yet fascinating to a child, and it grows so fast, it seems magical! To make it more fun, draw faces on the cups you plant in so the grass looks like hair when it grows!

⚬

Magical Wonders of Nature

Take bread to a pond and feed the ducks.

Help insects and birds find a new home by planting a tree...and explain it will also provide more oxygen for the neighborhood!

If there is no lightning or thunder, let your child stand out in a warm summer rain and actually catch raindrops on their tongue. Join them if you can be that adventurous. They'll love the experience even more!

If you don't hate the computer, look up the natural wonders of the world and discuss the amazing aspects of each with your children. Of course, books work just as well!

Plant a "butterfly bush." It will attract butterflies like crazy and provide entertainment for all of the children in your neighborhood!

Draw your child's attention to the buds of flowers before they bloom, so they can experience the birth of the flowers as the days go by. It makes flowers much more interesting.

Teach your children to appreciate the true beauty around them. The beauty of nature speaks to the soul, and to continue to call a child's attention to it is a precious gift to both of you.

Turn the radio, television, and any other noise off when driving in your vehicle, and encourage your children to enjoy the beauty around them in silence for three minutes.

Go on an "ABC Hike." Find a path in a local park or natural area and see how many different things your children can find that start with each letter of the alphabet.

Have a "Mini-Safari" scavenger hunt to look for some of the smaller details that are not always noticed in the natural world. Items that can be on the hunt list include: a spider's web, a caterpillar's cocoon, a leaf that has been nibbled by bugs, a drop of dew on a plant, a leaf with a fuzzy texture, and so forth. Add more items to the list that are appropriate for your environment.

Make a nature bracelet. Affix a tape "bracelet" to your child's arm by wrapping a piece of two-inch-wide masking tape loosely around their wrist with the sticky side out. As they see things that interest them such as leaves, sticks, dirt, and feathers, have them pick the items up and stick them onto the "bracelet." Remind them not to pick any live plants (or insects) for their decorations!

Take a "Micro-Hike." Have the kids "shrink down" to the size of an ant and crawl on their bellies along a micro-trail. Have them notice the micro differences between blades of grass, small rocks, etc. A magnifier or bug box can assist in their search.

Magical Wonders of Nature

Spray the hose so the water falls into an arc shape to the ground on a hot summer day. You should be able to create a rainbow, which will really make your children think you're magic!

❧

Host a neighborhood "Nature Day." Ask everyone on your block to plant something that day. It can be a simple flower or a tree in honor of nature's role in making your street a pleasant place to live.

❧

Hide some interesting stones and gems in the sand box (or table) for the children to find. Show them how to sift through the sand to find their little treasures.

❧

On a rainy day, set out a container to measure the rainfall. Ask your child to predict how much water will be collected. Measure how much rain fell that day and compare it to their answer. I bet they'll be surprised!

❧

Let your child "paint" with water. All you need is a paintbrush, a bucket of water, and a nice warm day. Paint rocks, trees, the sidewalk—anything! Watch how the water evaporates in the warm sun.

❧

Mommy Magic
Adria Manary

"Mother Nature"

—by Terry Lieberstein

I'm not a mom yet, but kids call me "Mother Nature." I've worked with children all over the country, introducing them to the wonders and joys of bugs, trees, animals, clouds, and many other amazing things found in the natural world.

I guess you could say that I'm certainly a "mom-in-training" working with so many wonderful children. Two of my favorites are my nephews, Jake and Sam. We've spent a lot of time exploring together. Our favorite activity is what we call nature road trips. Our road trips are sometimes short, sometimes long, and sometimes in-between. Whatever we happen to be curious about that day, we move out to explore…singing, telling stories, and playing as we drive. We have visited the beach to look for starfish in tide pools, the mountains to find fossils from millions of years ago; and even a quarry to examine rocks that were used by the local Native Americans to make paint.

The road trip that stands out in my mind was our visit to the local state park. Jake was eight and Sammy was five. We were walking down the path playing the ABC game (mentioned earlier in this chapter), when we turned the corner and there before us was a river. It was actually more of a creek, but to Jake and Sammy it was a RIVER. I've never seen two little boys get more excited! What could be more fun than a river with rocks of all different shapes and sizes on the banks?!

Sammy yelled, "Aunt Ter, can we throw some rocks into the river?"

"Well, sure you can. That's where they came from, and that's where they'll be washed back to," I replied with a smile. I couldn't help but think how nice it was to be outside where you can say "YES" a lot more often!

"Where will they end up?" asked Jake. "In the ocean?"

"That's right!" I said enthusiastically.

Then he said, "I guess everything ends up right where it belongs, doesn't it, Aunt Ter?"

Stunned into silence, I contemplated these wise words from my little nephew. I thought about how often I get too wrapped up in worrying about the future or the past...planning or regretting. And here the wisdom of the world spoke to me in the words of this wondrous child.

"Come on Aunt Ter, throw some rocks with us!" Sammy's little voice brought me back into the moment.

"Okay, boys, here we go!" I threw the first and largest rock into the water which splashed us all. The water fight that ensued that day was definitely recorded in our family history book.

The Power of the Mind

Teach children when they are young
The power of the mind,
And you will see the benefits
As they begin to find…

That if they will "THINK POSITIVE"
And if they will BELIEVE—
Then there truly is no limit
To what they can achieve!

Fill their minds with happy thoughts—
Be there to hold their hand.
Then with God's help they'll reach their goals
As they shout inside, "I CAN!"

The important thing is not so much that

every child should be taught, as that every

child should be given the wish to learn.

— John Lubbock

Mommy Magic
Adria Manary

7

The Magic of the Mind

The mind truly is a magical place where dreams are born and plans are conceived to make those dreams come true. If we take the time to fill our children's minds with positive thoughts, they will benefit from the seeds we sow for a lifetime. And if we teach them to visualize their goals at an early age—like professional athletes do—well, let's just say we might all be amazed!

One night my son Chase surprised me by telling me how he looked at his trophy shelf every night, and imagined a hockey trophy right in the middle! Hockey was his favorite sport, but almost every other sport was represented on his shelf except hockey. It was also the only sport he had played where the league only gave trophies to the top two teams—unlike the other sports, which gave participation trophies.

He visualized every night and played hockey every weekend. Finally, he had to go off to camp, and unfortunately had to miss the final two games. The team ended up receiving trophies, which were presented while he was gone. I picked his up, so it would indeed be sitting on his trophy shelf when he returned home. It's hard to describe the look on his face that night when he saw an actual trophy sitting right where he had imagined one!

One of my favorite stories is about the little girl whose mother took her tiny face into her hands every day, looked deep into her eyes, and said, "You have greatness within you." Of course the mother wondered if what she was trying to impart was actually understood by her young daughter. That is, until one day when she couldn't find her daughter. She looked and looked until she spied the closet door slightly ajar. Hearing her little girl's voice, she wondered to whom she was talking. As she moved toward the door, she noticed their dog was in the closet too. As she peeked in very quietly, she saw her precious little girl face-to-face with their German shepherd. Her daughter was holding the dog's huge face in her little hands and repeating the words she had heard so often, "Clyde," she said very seriously. "You have greatness within you."

Just as important as filling your child's mind with positive thoughts is teaching them to "speak their mind!" Letting them know that what they have to say is important will inspire them to stand up for what they believe in throughout their lives. In addition, communicating our thoughts in an articulate manner is an extremely important capability, and encouraging this in our children can give them a real head start.

When children start fighting physically, parents encourage them to "use their words," but nurturing their command of the language by teaching them to communicate their feelings effectively is the step sometimes missing. Take the time to help them find the words to best describe their frustration at times like these, as well as at other opportune moments . . . when something exciting happens or when someone hurts their feelings. Role-playing is also an excellent way to enhance your child's communication skills.

This chapter will offer a list of quotes to stimulate the mind of your child, either by quoting them directly or by paraphrasing them to impart important lessons. It will also offer a list of ways you can help your child to develop their mind—as well as communicate what's in it!

Whether you think that you can, or that you can't...
you are usually right.

— Henry Ford

We can all remember the famous sayings repeated over and over by our dear mothers...

"Eat all of your dinner; children are starving all over the world."

"Your mother knows best."

"Money doesn't grow on trees."

"Cleanliness is next to Godliness."

"Chew with your mouth closed."

The list goes on and on—but all of them had value and are pearls of wisdom from our pasts...even though we got tired of hearing them. As corny as it may seem, however, repetition is the mother of learning. Making sure we bestow powerful thoughts upon our children—even in the form of silly sayings or insightful quotes—is extremely valuable in

The Magic of the Mind

their learning processes. Here is a list to choose from when you need a little inspiration!

The first one is for you, Mom; and has always been one of my favorites:

> *Cleaning your house while your kids are still growing*
> *is like shoveling your walk before it stops snowing!*
>
> —Phyllis Diller

> *If you can't say something nice about someone,*
> *don't say anything at all.*
>
> —Anonymous

> *The important thing is to NOT stop questioning.*
>
> —Albert Einstein

> *Hitch your wagon to a star.*
>
> —Ralph Waldo Emerson

> *Only those who will risk going too far*
> *can possibly find out how far they can go.*
>
> —T.S. Eliot

> *You can do it!*
>
> —The cheer of every mother

You must do the thing that you think you cannot do.

—Eleanor Roosevelt

It is far better to be alone than to be in bad company.

—George Washington

You must first be a friend to have a friend.

—Anonymous

*It's better to have tried and failed
than never to have tried at all.*

—Anonymous

Look for the good in everything and you will find it.

—Anonymous

*The universe is full of magical things,
patiently waiting for our wits to grow sharper.*

—Eden Phillpotts

Goals that are not written down are just wishes.

—Anonymous

We are what we repeatedly do.
Excellence, therefore, is not an act but a habit.

—Aristotle

Habit is a man's best friend, or his worst enemy.

—Author Unknown

It's not only what you say, but how you say it.

—Anonymous

Am I not destroying my enemies when
I make friends with them?

—Abraham Lincoln

Obstacles are those frightful things you see
when you take your eyes off your goal.

—Henry Ford

One of the best things you can have up your sleeve...
is a funny bone!

—Author Unknown

Opportunities multiply as they are seized.

—Sun Tzu

Mommy Magic
Adria Manary

A pessimist sees the difficulty in every opportunity;
an optimist sees the opportunity in every difficulty.

−Sir Winston Churchill

The only thing necessary for the triumph of evil,
is for good men to do nothing.

−Edmund Burke

It's not the size of the dog in the fight;
it's the size of the fight in the dog!

−Mark Twain

Anger is a wind which blows out the lamp of the mind.

−Author Unknown

Children are likely to live up to what you believe of them.

−Lady Bird Johnson

He who sows courtesy reaps friendship,
and he who plants kindness gathers love.

−Author Unknown

Well-timed silence hath more eloquence than speech.

−Martin Fraquhar Tupper

The Magic of the Mind

The cost of a thing is that amount of life
which must be exchanged for it.

—Author Unknown

Wisdom begins in wonder.

—Socrates

A child prodigy is one with highly imaginative parents.

—Will Rogers

A candle's glow can pierce the darkest of night.

—Author Unknown

Proverbs:

He who lies down with dogs gets up with fleas.

One falsehood spoils a thousand truths.

Each person is his own judge.

He who learns, teaches.

Starting is the hardest part.

Exuberance is beauty.

Wheresoever you go, go with all your heart.

When you throw dirt, you lose ground.

If you are looking for a friend who has no faults,
you will have no friends.

He whose face gives no light shall never become a star.

Better to light a candle than to curse the darkness.

The more you appreciate it, the better it gets.

We will be known forever by the tracks we leave.

He who likes cherries soon learns to climb.

He is a good storyteller who can turn a man's ears into eyes.

The Magic of the Mind

A teacher will appear when the student is ready.

He whose hand gives, receives.

He who aims at nothing is sure to hit it.

He who helps someone up the hill gets closer to the top himself.

He who persists in knocking will succeed in entering.

As a man thinketh in his heart, so is he.

Encourage a child's perpetual sense of wonder. Buy a book like 101 Questions That Children Ask and be prepared to intelligently answer questions such as, "Why does a mosquito make you itch?" Sorry...I'm not giving the answer here, so get to the library...or easier yet, click on Google!

A joyful and secure atmosphere in the home provides the roots for self-esteem. In addition, although we must protect our children, it is not necessary to scare them. It is our duty as parents to keep the terrors of the world away from their minds until they are prepared to deal with the thoughts maturely. Be careful with what you watch on

Mommy Magic
Adria Manary

the news, for example. we do not allow inappropriate shows because of their rating, yet often what appears in the news is worse!

&

Have your children keep a dream journal. Whenever they have a desire to do something, have them write it down. Then as they get older, help them develop a plan to get there.

&

Children LOVE poetry. Recite it to them from an early age and they will be more likely to enjoy the art of writing it as they grow older. You can also use it to instill rules, phone numbers, and various ideals you would like to ingrain in their minds. Songs are also a good way of doing this. As mentioned earlier, I taught my daughter our phone number by singing the numbers to "Twinkle Twinkle Little Star." Another example is to sing the following words to the tune of "London Bridges Falling Down." "How can I be kind today, kind today, kind today? How can I be kind today? I will find a way."

&

Discuss events in the news that your child can understand and explain how they affect your family.

&

Be sure to include your children in some adult conversations. Ask for their opinions and really listen to their responses. You might be surprised at what you hear!

&

Once a week have your child memorize a verse, poem or short story depending on their age.

&

The Magic of the Mind

Have your child choose three cards out of a regular deck of cards and use them to: make the largest three-digit number; make the number that is closest to 500; make all possible even numbers; make all the numbers divisible by two, then four, then seven. For younger ones, have them simply lay them out from lowest to highest and vice versa.

❧

Play a game at the dinner table where your child pretends to be a television reporter, covering the events of that day. Take turns each night if you have more than one child, and join in on the fun on occasion as a guest reporter yourself! It will enhance their communication skills as well as provide wonderful entertainment after dinner. A spoon makes a great pretend microphone.

❧

Delight in the uniqueness of each of your children. With your encouragement they will not be afraid to be everything that they want to be!

❧

Mommy Magic
Adria Manary

Encouraging the Creative Mind

—by Linda O'Leary Sheetz

My daughter's first day of kindergarten was actually conducted as an "Open House Day" where both parents attended a "Teddy Bear Party." The children brought their favorite stuffed bears to introduce to the teacher. Then the teacher handed out copies of a cute little bear for the children to color.

As each child began to create their own little masterpieces, the mothers began chatting amongst themselves. Although deep in conversation, I was keeping an eye on my precocious daughter. I didn't think anything of the fact that she was holding her copied teddy bear picture up to the light and tracing her own version of the bear onto the reverse side of the paper. I knew she'd color it after she'd copied HER rendition of the picture onto the back.

However, the teacher was not in the mood to appreciate another way of approaching the assignment. I turned just in time to see her approaching my daughter with an angry and disapproving look on her face. I quickly stepped in, looked her straight in the eyes and said, "Isn't it incredible how creative Brianne is to have thought to hold the paper up to the light to trace a second bear onto the other side? Now she'll have two bears to color!" The teacher's face quickly softened as she said, "Oh my gosh, I never thought of it that way. I was just about to discipline her for not following my instructions."

Brianne proceeded to produce one of the most uniquely colored bears in the class. It was the perfect color scheme for what she felt represented her favorite bear.

I couldn't help but hope the teacher would be the one to learn the greatest lesson that day!

"There's Only ONE of Me!"

"There's only one of me!"
My child once squealed with glee,
As I told him how unique he was
And what he meant to me.

"No one has my nose!
And no one has my toes!
And NO ONE has MY mommy..."
Then the tears began to flow.

"Why, thank you," I then said.
As I laid him into bed.
Then I said a silent prayer
And kissed his tiny forehead.

It is a fact that every child is special.

Making them FEEL that way is one of

the most important aspects of parenting.

—Adria Manary

Mommy Magic
Adria Manary

There's Real Magic in Feeling Special

*I*f you tell your children they are special, they will believe you. If you tell your children they are not worthy, even inadvertently, they will also believe you. If they are splendid in your eyes, it is likely they will walk nobly out into the world.

When I was growing up, I was definitely the princess of the palace. My dad always called me his little princess—and one of my all-time favorite gifts from my parents was a pink "princess phone." (Please remember that this was the pre-cell phone era!) Only later did I learn the phone was actually put in my room for protection—in case of a fire, a burglar, or some such other problem since I was a "latchkey kid."

My parents did everything in their power to make me feel special growing up. And when it was out of their realm of power, they fought hard to convince others of the importance of their goal. I can remember when my big brother made the Little League baseball team, and my mom made sure I was the mascot—so I could wear a uniform too.

I also remember when she wouldn't take no for an answer when the Camp Fire Girls troop I desperately wanted to be in said they had enough girls for that particular group. How she got me in, I'll never know. She just said they couldn't turn down a special girl like me! What I really appreciated was that she got my best friend in as well.

I can also remember when I was *picked* to be my former first grade teacher's aide and was *paid* to help her after school. In actual fact, my mom had arranged this so I would be supervised after school for the half-hour between the time school got out and the time she arrived home from work.

They told me how I lit up a room when I entered it and how I had various special gifts. My mom told me I had "peaches and cream" skin, even in the midst of those difficult teenage years when my skin was a real problem for me.

My parents and brother were always the wind beneath my wings, and I feel that because of this I was thoroughly able to fly. What they said was sometimes true and sometimes not so true. The point is I believed what they said and lived up to their belief in me as best as I could.

We are all unique and have all been given special gifts. It is up to us as parents to help our children understand this so they will feel comfortable in traveling their own particular paths. We are all here for a reason. As difficult as life can get at times, if we hold on to that belief from childhood through adulthood, our lives will be filled with the happiness we were meant to enjoy.

Mommy Magic
Adria Manary

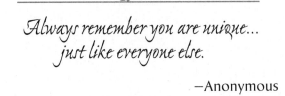

Always remember you are unique...
just like everyone else.

—Anonymous

Tell your child the story of the day they were born, and how there will never again be anyone born like them. If they are adopted, also tell them of the wonderful anticipation you felt just before they arrived and how much love and effort you put into finding them... and how they were meant to be with you.

❧

Special "dates" with Mommy and Daddy—separately. This is especially important if you have multiple children. This one-on-one time creates an environment where they feel comfortable in sharing feelings that might not otherwise come out in the normal, hectic pace of family schedules. It also creates distinct memories they will put into the treasure trove of their minds!

❧

Play "Positive Roundtable." Sit around the kitchen table (or around the edges of the hot tub like we prefer!) and take turns offering one thing each family member likes about the other members of the family. The first person says something they like about every family member, and then the next person does the same, and so on. Sometimes it's hard to get started, but once it gets going, the results are positive and heartfelt feelings abound for the whole family. If someone is having a difficult time thinking of something for a particular person, be sure to help them quickly so that person does not begin to feel bad.

&

Create acrostic poems using your children's names. Make them meaningful and loving. For example, I wrote the following one for my little girl, Astra:

A little girl who's such a pearl

So lovely in every way.

Tries her best to please the world

Reveling in every day.

An angel within her will always stay.

&

Make your child's birthday TRULY special...all day long. An example of such a day would be to start out by filling their room with balloons so they wake up to a celebration. Put a candle in their pancake, toast or waffle—whatever their choice is. Then have the other children in the family do one deed each to make the birthday child feel happy or special. Let them decorate their own cake—maybe a separate one if there is a need for a "perfect" one for the party. Make sure the school celebration is more than just cupcakes for the class if they're school age. A game about your child is often fun, with questions like, "What is Sally's favorite color?" Then the children who guess the correct answers can receive prizes, and the other children get to know her better! Let the evening's festivities include a treasure hunt for the birthday presents—which provides for a longer time in opening them than simply ripping off the paper! Remember to fix their favorite dinner and serve it by candlelight, or other creative lighting to create a unique atmosphere.

&

Mommy Magic
Adria Manary

Choose areas in which your child seems talented and make a point of telling them how gifted they are in those areas. Use phrases like, "You certainly are a talented artist!" or "The kindness you showed in sharing with your friend was very special," or "I have never seen a more interesting rock collection. Maybe you'll be an archeologist!" (And then explain what an archeologist is!)

❧

Make a family talent board, with pictures of each member doing what they do best—or maybe what they like to do best!

❧

Make sure you let your children eavesdrop sometimes when you're "bragging" about their accomplishments.

❧

Pick nicknames for each child that are special to Daddy and different ones that are special to Mommy.

❧

Remember, compliments are important, and much more special if they are specific.

❧

Children hear "no" seven times more often than they hear "yes." Explain you must say "no" because you care about their safety and well-being—and you wouldn't correct them if you didn't love them so much. In addition, find ways to say "yes" more often!

❧

There's Real Magic in Feeling Special

When they have achieved a particular accomplishment, hang a congratulatory sign up they will see as they come in the door and have a special snack waiting for them.

❦

Give flowers to your child. They're always picking dandelion bouquets for Mom, so return the favor! I'll never forget the enthusiastic, wide-eyed response of my four-year-old when I brought her flowers after her first recital. "FOR ME?!" she squealed. "These are the FIRST flowers I ever got!" Her joy penetrated my heart as she acted as though I had just given her a million dollars.

❦

Pull out old school work, pictures, cards, and other memorabilia and make a scrapbook together, all about your child. Discuss the value of each item as you place it into the book—describing how special the child is for having done such good work—and for having so many people who love them.

❦

Remember the dignity of your children. Never feel superior to them—because you are not.

❦

Stop self put-downs immediately! Sometimes children get into a bad habit of calling themselves names or putting themselves down, saying things like, "I wish I were as pretty as Annie," or "Why am I always so clumsy?!" Bring up their good points and then ask them to tell you three things they like about themselves. This should take the conversation in a more positive direction, and assure them they are special.

❦

Write letters to your child even if you're never apart. Writing your thoughts can be much different than speaking them, as it offers time for reflection. Write how you feel about them and how much you appreciate them. Compliment them on things they've done well. Leave the notes on their pillow, or somewhere they're sure to see them, or actually mail them. The words you write will be treasured by your children as they grow into their adult years.

❧

When your child's feelings are deeply hurt, or when he is completely embarrassed about something, declare the rest of the day: "Making [Child's Name] Feel Better Day!"

Have the whole family rally 'round! Buy them a special treat, have the other siblings write cards about what they like best about them, go out for ice cream, grant one simple wish they have expressed in the past. Ease the pain of your child while it is still within your control! As they grow older it will provide the understanding that they can ease their own pain—and possibly the pain of others.

❧

Encourage your child to be authentic...true to themselves. With the incredible amount of peer pressure that exists today, and the constant barrage of negative thinking that streams into our homes via internet and social media, television, our cars on the radio, and even into our schools in a variety of scary ways...start early in teaching your child to listen to his or her own heart and measure themselves by their own standards—not by comparing themselves to others.

❧

Make New Year's Day special by having a special story time around the fire—or wherever your special family gathering place may be. Tell a story about how important family is, and how families stick together through thick and thin. Offer examples like how one twig by itself can be broken easily...but when you bundle lots of twigs together, the strength increases dramatically. Then, instead of making resolutions like, "I'm going to lose ten pounds, I'm going to make more money, I'm going to stop smoking, the usual ones about yourself (although you can make those as well!)—try making a wish list or a goal list the entire family can be involved in. Your list might include projects to be done in the coming year, the best place for a vacation (vote on it and start planning it if possible), individual goals where family members agree to support and encourage the effort, or family goals such as having a garage sale where everyone gets to keep the money for the "stuff" they get out of their rooms!

Often your children will feel special because of something you have accomplished. Their mom baked the most delicious cookies, their dad has a cool car, their parents are very active in the community, or maybe their parents are famous in their jobs. Whatever the reason, let them share in the glory by helping you in some way, so they can feel like they are a part of it as well. I will never forget my very first book signing, when my kids signed their picture in the back of every book sold!

Help your children make others feel special sometimes. On Veteran's Day, I ask our children to write cards thanking their dad for helping to protect our country. My husband has been moved to tears at times by what they have written to him. He served in the Air Force for twenty years, was commissioned as an officer, and earned several medals. His accomplishments rarely come up since he is retired, but there was one time during our church service on the Sunday following Veteran's Day that will stay in my heart and mind forever. We had celebrated "his day" a few days before, and he had shared some stories about when he was in Vietnam. The kids had given him especially moving cards and were more aware of "war" having heard a lot about it since the fall of Iraq.

The pastor asked God to bless those in harm's way and then went on to thank those who had made our country safe in the past. She asked that any veteran who had served in a war stand in the congregation to be recognized. The kids urged their dad to stand, but they were not prepared for his reaction.

As others stood, there was absolute silence, and tears filled many of their eyes...including my husband's. The looks on my children's faces will stay with me for a very long time. It was as if they finally under-stood the seriousness of their dad's heroic efforts and the depth of the patriotism he felt. When the pastor then asked the family members to stand beside their loved ones, my children stood in honor of their dad, as if standing "at attention." It was a very proud and moving moment for our entire family.

❧

Completing chores is a perfect time to bring positive attention to your child. When they have completed a task, recognize how well it was done, and how not too many kids their age could have done such a great job!

❧

Give them periodic awards such as the one on the following page.

❧

There's Real Magic in Feeling Special

Best Children in the World Award for June to:

Chase Manary

For Good behavior in the following areas:

-1-

For an EXCELLENT report card and making us VERY PROUD
with his school awards.

-2-

Taking such good care of his sister at
Universal Studios and the Fair.

-3-

Making his bed every day.

-4-

Taking the trash out, without having to be asked.

-5-

Doing chores when asked without exasperation!

-6-

For his sensitivity in showing his mother
a great deal of compassion.

Mommy Magic
Adria Manary

Still Special...After All These Years

—by Sandi Bruegger

*M*y mom was a freshman in high school when she was thrown into the "real world" of marriage and motherhood. The marriage did not last and she soon moved to California in search of better things for herself and her new family. I chose to stay behind with my father, and have remained here for the last twenty years. Because of the thousands of miles between mom and me, as well as the heartache, there was always a distance between us both physically and emotionally.

I met a wonderful man named John one fall, and by winter we were married. A few short weeks later, we learned of our pregnancy. There is always a part of you, no matter what age or situation, that feels the need to have the approval of your parents. This was a situation in which I knew I would never find that approval, however. My mom had always wanted my life to be better than hers. By that she meant I was to get a degree, be an independent career woman and maybe start a family in my thirties. She "could not" be a grandmother before age fifty! She was thirty-six when I became pregnant.

When I finally built up the courage to give her the news, she reacted exactly as I had anticipated and feared—with utter disappointment. I hung up the phone, angry and hurt, determined she would never be a part of our lives. After all, we had family close by that supported our baby and us. We'd be fine. We didn't need her. But a teary little girl's voice in my mind whispered, "Yes...we do."

We didn't speak often, but soon the packages began to arrive. First a few small things came, and then finally a crib and changing table set. I think it was the only way she knew how to say that she accepted her new role as Grandma, and that she had begun to respect my role as a mother.

When I went into premature labor at twenty-seven weeks, I attempted to reach her by phone, but to no avail. I finally was forced to leave a message on her machine, figuring that it would not be returned. The little girl inside of me was devastated. I lay in the hospital bed for hours, connected to countless IVs and monitors. I trembled constantly from all of the drugs, and was terrified that my child's wellbeing was in danger. "I WANT MY MOMMY!" I screamed inside of my head. I fought the urge to dial her number again. John left to get a soda and I tried to concentrate on the steady blips that were my baby's heartbeat.

The sound of slow, reluctant feet entered my room. Sure that it was John taking his time getting back, I barked for him to hurry up. A hesitant hand reached up and slid the curtain aside. I had to blink the haze away several times, just to be sure I was seeing right. "IT'S MOMMY! MOMMY'S HERE—MOMMY'S HERE!" I cried inside of my heart. The little girl inside wanted to dance and sing. My mother stood there for a moment, tears in her eyes, unable to speak. And when she finally did manage the words—I learned a lesson in motherhood that I will carry with me for the rest of my life: "Remember, they just never stop being your baby."

Mommy Magic
Adria Manary

Yummy Smells

Deep in my heart
Where my memories dwell,
Lives my mom in an apron
And yummy smells.

I'm thankful for cookies
And chocolate cake,
For when I smell these
Those images awake.

I am taken back in time
As I close my eyes,
And can almost taste the cookies
My mom baked with pride.

"Can I lick the bowl?"
My little one squeals!
I'm jerked back to the present
By his wonderful zeal.

I look at his face
All chocolate and smiles,
And know that this moment
Will last him a good while.

The kitchen is always

the happiest room in the house.

—Anonymous

Mommy Magic
Adria Manary

Cooking Up Some Magic

Our sense of smell has the power to evoke memories in an instant. Memories that were otherwise far from thought are conjured up so clearly that we are mentally jolted back to another time. The smell of oatmeal chocolate chip cookies in the oven takes me back to my mom's kitchen...watching her, helping her, and waiting to eat the results. And when I eat pineapple upside-down cake, although I've never tasted another one as good as my mom made, I am still overwhelmed by a warm and cozy memory that I hope is never lost.

In writing this book, however, I had not included the importance of "kitchen magic" because, quite honestly, I am not a great cook! Fortunately, through the suggestion of a friend, and subsequent urgings from other mothers, I realized what an oversight that was and included this chapter.

One fact that has remained true throughout the history of the home is that the kitchen has always been the center of activity. With the fast-paced society we live in today, it is often at the kitchen table that we have our most insightful discussions and important family times. Even at parties, guests seem to gravitate toward the kitchen!

From holiday cooking, birthday cakes, and fresh baked bread—to Jell-O jigglers and microwave cooking—making magic in the kitchen is a fun way to bond with your children and create memories that will last a lifetime.

In this chapter we offer several fun recipes that are "children friendly" and mother approved! Of course, all recipes meet these requirements if you simply take the time to include your children in the fun. Often the simple act of letting your child crack the eggs can be the beginning of a plethora of enjoyable activities that will delight your children.

> *Non-cooks think it's silly to invest two hours' work into two minutes' enjoyment, but if cooking is evanescent, so is the ballet.*
>
> —Julia Child

Friendship Bread

The most important ingredient in this treat is FRIENDS! If you are starting this recipe without a bag of batter along with it, be sure to start at step six. Do NOT use a metal spoon or bowl for mixing, and do NOT refrigerate. If air gets into the bag, let it out. A one-gallon Ziploc is best. It's normal for the batter to thicken, bubble and ferment. Here are the day-by-day instructions:

Day 1   This is the day you receive the batter. Do nothing.
Day 2   Squeeze the bag.
Day 3   Squeeze the bag.
Day 4   Squeeze the bag.
Day 5   Squeeze the bag. (Kids are great squeezers!)
Day 6   Add 1 cup all purpose flour, 1 cup sugar, and 1 cup milk to

the bag.

Day 7   Squeeze the bag.

Day 8   Squeeze the bag.

Day 9   Squeeze the bag.

Day 10   Combine in a large bowl: batter, 1 cup flour, 1 cup sugar, 1 cup milk. Mix with a wooden spoon or spatula. Pour four 1 cup starters in Ziploc bags. Keep one starter for yourself, and give the other three to your friends along with a copy of these instructions.

Still on Day 10...Add the following to the batter remaining in the bowl: 1 cup oil, 1 cup sugar, 1 teaspoon vanilla, 3 large eggs, 1/2 teaspoon baking powder, 1/2 teaspoon salt, 2 cups all-purpose flour, 1/2 cup milk, 1/2 teaspoon baking soda, 1 large box instant vanilla pudding, 2 teaspoons cinnamon. Pour the batter into 2 large well-greased and sugared loaf pans. You can sprinkle some extra cinnamon and sugar on top. Bake at 350°F for 60 minutes.

Mommy Magic
Adria Manary

Easy Forest Torte Cake

1 package Duncan Heinz Devils Food cake mix
1 package (3 ounce) cherry Jell-O
3/4 cup boiling water
1/2 cup cold water
3 tablespoons cherry liqueur (optional)
1 package (4 1/2 or 4 3/4 ounce) instant pudding
2 envelopes Dream Whip topping mix
1 1/4 cups cold milk
1 can (21 ounce) cherry pie filling

Prepare cake mix according to package directions, using two 9" round cake pans. A few minutes before the cake is done (follow the cooking time on the package), start boiling a 3/4 cup of water and mix with Jell-O until completely dissolved. Next add the 1/2 cup cold water and the cherry liqueur. (The liqueur is optional. You can just add an additional 3 tablespoons of water if you prefer.) Le Croix cherry brandy is a good choice. When cake has cooled about 5 minutes, remove layers to two separate dinner plates. Poke holes in both layers with tines of a fork. Next, slowly spoon the Jell-O mixture over both layers until all is absorbed. Cover layers with plastic wrap and refrigerate for two hours or overnight.

Cooking Up Some Magic

When ready to frost, combine pudding mix, topping mix and milk in a small bowl. Beat at medium speed for 2–3 minutes. Using 1 cup pudding mixture, make a 1" high and wide ring around the outer edge of the top of one layer. Spoon the cherry pie filling into the center of this "corral," reserving about three cherries. Remove second layer from plate with a spatula and gently settle it on top of the bottom layer. Frost with pudding mixture, swirling it with your knife. Finally, put remaining three cherries on the top center. Refrigerate until ready to serve.

This is a fun and rewarding cake to make with your children. It is so delicious and you and your child will receive so many compliments that they will feel a real sense of accomplishment. Using a box mix makes this a user-friendly recipe. Moms with little time and little cooking experience will find this is a no-fail recipe. The children love poking the holes in the cake and can do no harm ladling the Jell-O mixture any old way. Spooning the pretty cherries into the center of the cake is easy and fun, particularly when a few cherries miss the cake and meet a little mouth. Making swirls in this stiff frosting is easy and pretty. Finally, the chance for beater and spoon licking is a delight. You end up with chocolate chins and great big grins.

Mommy Magic
Adria Manary

Pumpkin Pancakes

If your kids like pumpkin pie they'll love these!

2 cups Bisquick

1 egg

1 1/2 cups milk

1/2 cup solid packed pumpkin

1 teaspoon cinnamon

1/2 teaspoon nutmeg

1 tablespoon sugar

1 spray can of whipping cream

Mix all together (more milk if necessary to make it the consistency of a regular pancake mixture). Pour onto griddle, desired size. (Remember silver dollar size is fun.) Serve with whipped cream. (And let the kids squirt the cream!)

Homemade Wontons

1 pound ground turkey
1 egg
1/2 cup green onion
1 1/2 tablespoons soy sauce
1 tablespoon cornstarch
1/2 tablespoon sesame oil
3 shitake mushrooms, minced
A pinch of sugar
1 package wonton wrappers

Mix all together. Stir until blended. Lay wonton wrappers out and put 1/2 teaspoon of mixture into each one. From here follow directions on wonton package to fold. Boil a medium-sized pot of water. Cook the folded wontons 3–5 minutes. Drain and rinse. To serve, boil chicken broth and add desired amount of wontons. Boil 2 minutes. Pour into bowls and sprinkle with more sliced onion if desired.

These are so fun to make, and kids love to eat them!

Rice Krispy Treats with a Twist

(Double recipe)
1/2 cup butter or margarine plus an extra tablespoon
80 marshmallows
10 cups Rice Krispies cereal
1/2 cup peanut butter
1 cup chocolate chip morsels

Grease a 13x9x2 pan. Add chocolate morsels with a tablespoon of butter. Heat (best in microwave but don't use a metal pan) until morsels are slightly melted. Stir and smooth thin coat of chocolate across bottom of pan. Next, heat remaining butter in large saucepan over low heat. Add marshmallows, stirring until melted, and then add peanut butter. Remove from heat, add cereal and stir until evenly coated. Press mixture into baking pan (use wax paper or spoon). Refrigerate until chocolate is hardened. Cut into 2x2 squares.

Edible and Easy Finger Paint

Light corn syrup
Food coloring (liquid works best)
Paper plates for mixing
Newsprint or other paper for painting
For each portion, pour 1 tablespoon corn syrup onto paper plate.
Squirt food coloring into the puddle. Mix and paint with fingers.

Mommy Magic
Adria Manary

Fortune Cookies

4 egg whites
1 cup sugar
1/2 cup plain flour
1/2 cup melted butter
1/4 teaspoon salt
1/2 teaspoon vanilla essence
2 tablespoons water
NON-TOXIC pen
Strips of plain white paper

Preheat oven to 350°F. Write down fortunes or messages on small strips of paper and fold them in half. (You can have a lot of fun with funny ones.) Mix the sugar and the egg whites and blend melted butter into the sugar mixture. Stir until the mixture is smooth. Grease a cookie sheet very well and pour the batter from a spoon to form circles around 2" in diameter.

NOTE: *These cookies will spread, so space them far apart so they do not join together. Cook for approximately 10–15 minutes and then remove from oven.*

Place messages/fortunes on top of the warm cookie and fold the cookie over, and then over again, forming the fortune cookie shape. Cookies cool quickly and hold their shape.

Grandma's Orange Cookies

1 cup shortening

2 cups sugar

2 eggs

1 orange (squeeze the juice, and grate the rind,
reserving 2 tablespoons of juice for the icing)

4 cups flour

1 teaspoon salt

1 teaspoon baking soda

2 teaspoons baking powder

1 cup buttermilk

Preheat oven to 400°F. Cream shortening and sugar thoroughly. Add eggs and beat well. Add orange juice and grated rind, mix well. In measuring cup, add soda to buttermilk. Combine flour, baking powder and salt. Alternate adding buttermilk and flour combinations by thirds, to creamed mixture. Mix well after each addition. Drop by tablespoons onto greased cookie sheet and bake for 10 minutes, or until the edges are barely brown. Allow to cool completely before adding icing.

Icing

    2 cups powdered sugar

    2 tablespoons margarine

    Dash of salt

    2 tablespoons orange juice

Mix all together until smooth. Top each cookie. Icing will set up in a few minutes to allow you to stack the cookies in a container.

Mommy Magic
Adria Manary

Candy Bar Pie

Ingredients for the crust:

  2 cups all-purpose flour

  1 teaspoon salt

  2/3 cup shortening

  1 tablespoon cold butter

  4–5 tablespoons ice-cold water

Combine flour and salt in a bowl. Cut in shortening and butter until particles are the size of small peas. Sprinkle with water, one tablespoon at a time, mixing lightly with a fork until all the flour is moistened. Gather into a ball. Divide into two equal parts and enclose each in plastic wrap. Flatten each piece to a 5" pancake size disk.

Chill in the refrigerator for 30 minutes.

Roll out one piece into a circle 1/8" thick. Roll out the dough on a pastry cloth to eliminate using extra flour. (Extra flour creates a tougher crust.) Place crust in a 9" glass pie shell. Flute the edge for a decorative touch.

The other piece of pastry dough can be made into another piecrust or rolled out and cut into pastry cutouts to decorate the top of the finished pie.

Place the pastry cutouts on a cookie sheet. Brush with milk or cream and sprinkle sugar on the top. Bake at 400°F for 8–10 minutes.

Ingredients for the filling:

3 eggs, slightly beaten
3/4 cup white corn syrup
1/2 cup brown sugar, firmly packed
1/4 cup melted butter
1/4 teaspoon salt
1 teaspoon vanilla
1 cup chopped pecans
1 1/2 cups chopped candy bars (12 small bars of milk chocolate, caramel, nougat or peanut)
One 9" unbaked piecrust
Whipped cream
Pastry cutouts of small leaves or pumpkins
Slices of candy bars

Combine the first six ingredients in a bowl. Stir in the chopped pecans and chopped candy bars. Pour into an unbaked piecrust. Bake at 375°F for 40–55 minutes or until a knife inserted halfway between the center and the edges comes out clean.

When the top of the pie is the desired shade, cover the top loosely with foil to prevent further browning. Cool pie on a rack. When pie is cool, garnish the top with whipped cream, pastry cutouts and candy bar slices.

Mommy Magic
Adria Manary

Easy Bake Oven Pretty Pink Cake

I was very happy to find this recipe since we loved to use our Easy Bake Oven, but didn't always have the pre-packaged mixes in the cupboard!

5 tablespoons cake flour
1/4 teaspoon baking powder
A pinch of salt
5 teaspoons red sugar crystals
1/4 teaspoon vanilla extract
4 teaspoons vegetable oil
8 teaspoons milk

Stir together cake flour, baking powder, salt, red sugar, vanilla, oil, and milk until batter is smooth and pink. Pour 3 tablespoons of batter into greased and floured cake pan. Bake 15 minutes. Repeat for second layer.

Frosting:

4 teaspoons shortening
2/3 cup powdered sugar

1/4 teaspoon vanilla
2 teaspoons milk
Colored sugar crystals

Stir together shortening, powdered sugar, vanilla, and milk until smooth and creamy. Spread 2 teaspoons of frosting on top of the first layer. Add second layer and continue frosting. Sprinkle with colored sugar.

Mommy Magic
Adria Manary

Miniature Gingerbread House

This is a craft project with food—yum! When you don't have time to make a full gingerbread house...

7 graham crackers
Frosting for glue (recipe below)
Assorted small candies for decorating
Ribbon
Frosting:
1/2 pound confectioner's sugar
3 tablespoons butter/margarine
1/2 teaspoon vanilla
1 1/2–2 tablespoons milk

Mix all the ingredients together until smooth and spreadable, not runny. Add more sugar if too runny.

If you have a pastry bag, place frosting in bag and use a small tip. If not, you can use a zip lock bag, cutting a small whole in the corner.

Place one graham cracker flat on the table; squeeze a little frosting around all edges. You may need an extra pair of hands!

Place one cracker on each side standing up (it now looks like a box with no top.)

Carefully squeeze more frosting on all outside corners, top to bottom and around the bottom of the box.

Let stand for a short while to let frosting harden a little. This will make working with the roof a little easier.

Now squeeze frosting on two of the top edges of the box and place the last two graham crackers on the roof forming an inverted "V". It now looks like a triangle on a box from the side and may overhang if you can get the frosting to hold for you.

Squeeze frosting along the top of the roof where crackers join. Let stand again until frosting hardens a little.

Now comes the fun part: With leftover frosting, cover the roof to look like snow (two sides are left open). Then, squeezing small amounts on candy, place candy on the house to decorate. You can use the frosting to add things like doors and windows. Just use your imagination.

After the project is totally dry, string ribbon through to open side of the roof and hang on Christmas tree.

If you want to do this project with young children, you might want to make the base house ahead of time, gluing the corners from the inside—and let it harden. Then turn them loose with frosting and small candies to do the decorating.

Special Note: This craft is safe to eat, but if you would like to save your treasure for years to come, you can use a spray varnish in a well-ventilated area. (2–3 coats of varnish).

Mommy Magic
Adria Manary

*With so many goodies, I guess we should throw in
a few good, solid (yet easy) meals!*

Honey Ginger Grilled Salmon

1 teaspoon Ground Ginger
1 teaspoon Garlic Powder
1/3 cup soy sauce
1/3 cup orange juice
1/4 cup honey
1 green onion, chopped
1 1/2 pounds salmon fillet

In a large self-closing plastic bag, combine first six ingredients; mix well. Place salmon in bag and seal tightly. Turn bag gently to distribute marinade.

Refrigerate 15 minutes or up to 30 minutes for stronger flavor. Turn bag occasionally.

Lightly grease grill rack. Preheat grill to medium heat. Remove salmon from marinade; reserve the marinade. Grill 12–15 minutes per inch of thickness or until fish flakes easily with a fork. Brush with reserved marinade up until the last 5 minutes of cooking time. Discard leftover marinade.

Calzone Pronto

1 tablespoon olive oil
1/2 sliced mini-peppers (not the hot variety—just small bell pep-
　　pers in a variety of colors)
1/2 cup chopped red onion
2 cloves minced garlic
3 precooked sausages, sliced
1 pound fresh pizza dough
1 cup grated cheese

Preheat oven to 450°F. Sauté peppers, onions and garlic in oil. When
the vegetables are fragrant, add sausages. Brown the meat and remove
from pan to cool ingredients before placing on dough.

Roll out pizza dough into a large rectangle. Sprinkle a layer of cheese
on the dough. Add the meat mixture and sprinkle again with cheese.

Lap each end of the dough over the middle, sealing edges. Slash the
top with a sharp knife so the steam can escape. Bake for 20 minutes
until golden brown.

Tuscan Chicken

4 skinless, boneless chicken breast halves
1 (4 ounce) can sliced black olives, drained
1 (15 ounce) can cannellini beans, rinsed and drained
1 (26.5 ounce) can roasted garlic flavored spaghetti sauce

Preheat the oven to 400°F. Coat a 9x13 inch baking dish with non-stick cooking spray. Place the chicken breasts in the baking dish, and sprinkle olives over the top. Pour the beans over the chicken, then pour the spaghetti sauce over everything.

Cover and bake for 30 minutes in preheated oven. Remove the cover and continue baking for 10 minutes, or until chicken is no longer pink inside.

Nachos

1 14 ounce bag tortilla chips
1 1/2 cups salsa
2 cups shredded cheddar cheese
6 ounce olives
2 cans of refried beans

Preheat oven to 400°F. Spread refried beans on baking sheet, then put the tortilla chips on top of the beans. Using a spoon, spread salsa over tortilla chips. Sprinkle cheese and olive pieces on top of tortilla chips. Bake for about 5 minutes. Remove from oven, let cool slightly, and dig into your nachos!

Mommy Magic
Adria Manary

The Kitchen Magnet

—by Val Acciani

*W*e have kitchen magnets all over our refrigerator that hold priceless works of art, schedules, photos of happy times. Doesn't every mother? However, the "kitchen magnet" I am referring to here is the actual kitchen AS the magnet.

My two vivacious little boys are always on the go...but when I go into the kitchen, my littlest one drops everything and is right on my heels. "Can I stir, Mommy?" was, I believe, the first sentence he ever put together. He had the motivation to use his words because he wanted to help mommy so badly. I will always call him "my little chef."

Fond memories of special times in the kitchen with my own mom has been motivation for me to continue the same traditions with my children. When I was around ten years old I went through a difficult period of being the brunt of teasing at school. I would come home in tears almost every day, and there my mom would be in the kitchen with ingredients for something yummy ready for me to help create. The concoctions took my mind off my problems, and the time without radio or television gave my mom ample opportunity to hear what was wrong and share her wisdom with me. We shared many a healing moment in that kitchen, and the bonding that took place over flour, eggs and sugar was a happy circumstance.

I now understand the many other reasons why these sessions were so important to my mom. Watching as my oldest counts out eighty marshmallows like a little miser and then squashes them all, gleefully turning back into the little boy I know, is a good example. Or letting my littlest crack the eggs (even though there may very well be a shell in the cake) and then watching as he walks like a monster to the sink, his hands covered in goo. And of course, the many happy, chocolate-covered faces!

The biggest reason I love our "kitchen time" is the special bonding that has occurred as a result of it. Holiday cooking is great, but when you make it an ongoing team effort, the fun is immeasurable!

Mommy Magic
Adria Manary

The Secret of Kindness

Kindness is the secret
To a person's peace of mind.
Practice it on everyone
And you will always find...

Your own heart will be lightened
And your soul will be at peace,
Even more than those you comfort
And those whose pain you cease.

So make a moment happier
For someone in your life
And make the world a better place
Where kindness conquers strife.

Sometimes the world seems scary,
Sometimes it seems so cruel.
But love can shine through darkness
If we mind the golden rule.

Kindness in words creates confidence.

Kindness in thinking creates profoundness.

Kindness in giving creates love.

—Lao-Tzu

Mommy Magic
Adria Manary

Magic Manners

$\mathcal{I}$t is apparent these days most parents and schools are doing a wonderful job teaching children to say please and thank you. After all, these are the "magic words." What is often missing, however, is an emphasis on the importance of courtesies and acts of kindness that go beyond these surface niceties. "Say the magic word," is heard over and over in kitchens and schoolrooms across America. What needs to be added is a reminder to *perform* the magic of kindness as well.

In the "old days," having good manners meant more than just saying the right words. It meant not letting a door slam into the face of the person behind you, for example. Or making sure someone was included in a conversation. Or watching children as they walked to school to see who might be left behind, and then encouraging the other children to walk with them the next day.

In a society that revolves around the great rat race, it was bound to happen. We have finally given in to the rats! I'm not referring to the problem of overpopulation. What I am referring to is the fact that the "rats" are taking over—in droves. They have been underground for a long time, eating away at our values and beliefs. But now they have gained enough momentum (and support through apathy) that they are rearing their ugly heads in public every day.

I truly believe, as parents, the responsibility lies with us to rise up against the darkness pervading our society. The light of love is our best weapon, and every beam of kindness that shines from our hearts is a step toward brightening the world, especially for our children... and their children. Leading by example is the best way to bring about change and to teach our children the Golden Rule.

One of my favorite quotes about the true essence of a mother, as well as a wonderful example of the ultimate in social graces, is from Tenneva Jordan, who once said:

> *A mother is a person who, seeing there are only four pieces of pie for five people, promptly announces that she never did care for pie.*

As moms, we make many sacrifices for our children; one of which is turning down invitations. This may be far down the sacrificial list (after giving up much needed sleep and those many pieces of pie which, quite honestly, would have been scrumptious), but it is still notable. How many shopping dates have we declined in order to take our children to a playgroup or baseball practice? How often have we chosen a Chuck E. Cheese party over a wine and cheese party? Needless to say, I am sure we have enjoyed those choices, and we understand the value of the time we spend with our children. However, what I heard the one day confirmed for me that in parenting, the rewards reaped by following the Golden Rule are priceless.

My daughter and I had planned to go to the movies one Friday night when my husband was away on business and my two boys were spending the night with friends. We were deciding which movie to see when the phone rang. As I handed the phone to her, I knew our evening with "just us girls" was slipping away. I continued to peruse the movie choices, thinking I would now be going solo since I knew what the call was about. Every Friday, her friend (now on the phone) goes ice-skating, and often invites Astra. As I listened to the conversation, that was indeed the reason for her call.

Mommy Magic
Adria Manary

What I heard next, however, was a very pleasant surprise.

"No, I can't," Astra said.

She listened as her friend undoubtedly tried to convince her to go—and most likely, advised her to "beg" me for the "yes" answer they both usually wanted.

However, what my precious daughter said next was truly a gift.

"No really—this is my decision. I don't want to 'ditch' my mom. We planned to go to the movies together and if I go ice-skating, she'll be all alone."

The "mom" in me was prompted to say, "It's okay honey, you can go." But fortunately for both of us, the little girl in me held my lips tightly together. I just sat there, silently basking in the glow of my daughter's choice of turning down her other invitation to go with me!

The rest of the evening was absolutely delightful. We laughed together, cried together, ate cinnamon pretzels, and drank cherry Icees as we watched one of our now-favorite movies, The Polar Express. At the end of the movie, Santa declares that the true magic of Christmas lies in your heart. That evening was a perfect example.

There is definite magic in being kind and having good manners. It can turn an otherwise gloomy day into one where the sunshine of your kindness has cast its rays into the life of someone less fortunate. It can simply make a person feel good. It can change a person's attitude toward you in a split second. It can open the door to opportunity. It will enhance your world and the world of those around you. The possibilities are endless.

In this chapter the suggestions and ideas will help you to show your children the importance of being kind, as well as the magic that kindness can bring into everyone's lives.

Mommy Magic
Adria Manary

A loving heart is the truest wisdom.

—Charles Dickens

Whenever your child exhibits an act of kindness, don't just acknowledge it, but also ask them how it made them feel. "Doesn't it feel good inside when you show kindness?" is a good phrase to use.

Pick a cause that appeals to the family, and do something to support it at least once a month. A few examples might be to take your pet to a nursing home, serve a meal at a homeless shelter, or sponsor a child through Save the Children or World Vision—not only sending money, but also letters and pictures from the family.

Watch your children as they walk to school or to the bus. If a child in the neighborhood is always walking behind, encourage your child to think of something to talk to them about and walk with them sometimes.

Always say hello in an elevator.

Encourage your children to offer at least one sincere compliment a day.

If you ever go to a poverty-stricken area such as Tijuana, Mexico, give your children bags of small apples they can hand out to the needy children. My family did this and it was one of the best experiences we've ever had that showed our children the value of small gifts to others. My heart swelled as I watched my little "pied pipers" handing out apples to these sad and needy urchins. As we walked through the downtown area, still being followed by expectant youngsters, my son said something far beyond his years. "You know what, Mommy? Some people want to be rich so bad...and if they came down here, they'd realize that they are already rich!" He gave me goose bumps (or angel bumps as I like to call them)—and he learned a valuable lesson.

❧

Teach your children good telephone manners. Think about what a welcome surprise it is when you call a friend and the child answers with good manners. Phrases like, "May I ask who's calling?" and, "Just one moment please" are simple—yet will set your children apart as children who have shown good manners.

❧

Remember—a kindness a day keeps your own blues away.

❧

Teach your children to encourage others rather than discourage them.

❧

Have your children become "door monitors." Every time they go through a door, explain that a good door monitor looks behind to make sure the door does not shut on someone coming up behind them.

❧

Have your children write thank-you notes for special acts of kindness shown to them—as well as for presents.

If an elderly person lives in the neighborhood, suggest your child help them once a week by taking out their trash, raking leaves, shoveling their driveway, or attending to a special need they may have.

Encourage kindness between siblings. Suggest they each do something nice for each other at least once a week that is above and beyond their normal behavior. Perhaps they could do their sister's chore because she has a project due at school the next day.

Have Daddy help the children to understand ways they can be kind to Mommy. Perhaps playing quietly when she has a headache or offering to perform a chore without being asked. How about helping Mom carry the groceries?

Put out a bird feeder to make the winter easier for our little feathered friends.

Teach your children to look for ways to show kindness. These could include things like helping a senior citizen into the car, offering to carry something for a person whose arms are full, offering their seat to an elderly person or a pregnant woman, or helping a mother with a stroller through a door.

Be a good example. If you are kind to others– so shall your children be.

Take flowers to a nursing home and have your child pick a resident to present them to.

Ask your child about the kids in their class. If there is someone who seems unpopular, encourage your child to be particularly nice to them– and protect them from the mean remarks of others.

Have your children pick out toys they no longer use and instead of just taking them to a collection place, take them directly to an orphanage so they can see the happy faces of the recipients.

Tell your children how much you love their smiles–and how important it is to smile at the people around them.

Pack some extra goodies in your child's lunch box to share.

If someone new moves into the neighborhood, have your child come with you to welcome them with a fruit basket or flowers from your garden. And if there are children, have your child show them where the park is, and help them get used to the neighborhood.

Remind your children to always return a favor.

Mommy Magic
Adria Manary

My son's fourth grade teacher had the whole class write down what they liked about each child in the class. Only good comments were allowed. On the last day of school, she presented each child's list of compliments to them. It was a very positive experience for the kids. Ask your child's teacher to try this.

Although it is important for children to understand that performing an act of kindness will be returned tenfold, it is also important they understand the act in itself is what brings joy to the heart.

We all know how hard it is for children to share, so make an effort to show them how special they are when they do well in sharing with their friends. Before a friend comes over to play, have a little talk with your child and explain that you understand how hard it is for them to share their toys, and it is something very hard for all children. So, if they share freely, it will be like a surprise for their friends! And if they share well during their playtime, you will share a surprise with them after the friend leaves!

Encourage your children to see through the eyes in their heart...as well as the eyes in their head.

Teach your children early that a promise is a promise.

Mommy Magic
Adria Manary

Furby Has A Heart

—by Letitia Baldridge

At the height of the "Furby" craze, during the holiday season, I happened to be standing in a toy store on New York's chic Upper East Side, awaiting my turn in line. Over in the corner, just watching, was a homeless mother, bare-legged, dirty, and disheveled. I think she was in the store to keep warm, or maybe it was simply to allow her daughter to look at all of the toys. Her child watched the other children lined up with their mothers, fathers, and caregivers, anxiously waiting to buy one of the coveted talking Furbies. Once or twice she said in a soft voice, "I'd really like one of those, too." Her mother quietly shushed her and told her not to be crazy; of course she could not have one. The little girl's face grew sadder and sadder as she watched each furry character walk out of the store with someone else.

One of the private school girls, around ten years old, dressed in her pristine school uniform, saw and heard the little girl. When her mother finally received the treasured, wrapped Furby, she handed it to her daughter and paid the salesperson. As they walked out of the store, her daughter went over to the homeless mother's child, put the package in her hands, and said, "This is for you." Then she hurried out of the store after her mother.

Tears came to my eyes. I had spent so much time writing about the need for children to develop a kind heart, about how we, as adults, should show them the way—and then I see a naturally and wonderfully kind child do an act right from her heart. There had been no suggestion from her mother that she give away her new Furby. There had been no conversation at all about it. She simply saw a peer with no chance whatsoever to own a Furby, it touched her, and she reacted.

That child has what it takes to go a long way in this world. From what I witnessed, I feel confident she will achieve fame, fortune and success in every way...but most of all, happiness. Kindness was in her heart, but surely her mother, father, or someone at home helped put that kind of philosophy there. It just doesn't happen automatically, but how wonderful it would be if it were contagious.

The Golden Lesson for Our Children

When children are respected
They learn to respect.
When children are disrespected
They learn to disrespect.
When children are loved
They learn to love.
When children are unloved
They learn emptiness and don't know how to love.
When children are nurtured
They learn to nurture.
When children are treated unfairly
They treat others unfairly.
When children are disciplined with respect
They will discipline their future children with respect.
When children's possessions are treated with respect
They learn to treat others' possessions with respect.
When children see their parents respect others
They will respect others.

Truly…it is as simple as that.

As a child, my family's menu consisted of two choices:

take it or leave it!

—Buddy Hackett

Mommy Magic
Adria Manary

11

The Magic of Respect...
The Secret of Discipline

*R*especting our children, and teaching them to respect others is second only to loving them.

In writing this chapter, I thought about my own upbringing. Why had my brother and I not rebelled as much—or as drastically—as some of our friends? The one thing that still rings in my ears is the reason my mother gave to a neighbor who once asked what her "secret" was to raising such wonderfully caring and polite children. (It still feels good when I think about that compliment.) My mother responded with one word: respect. How many times had she told me, "Respect goes both ways, sweetheart. I will respect you...if you respect me." No truer words were ever spoken. It was her version of the Golden Rule, and it put an alarm off in my mind whenever I started to do something that might cause her to lose respect for me. Of course, she disciplined me when the alarm did not ring loudly enough in my head and I did something wrong, but it was the basis for my desire to be "good."

Children want and need limits; a truth of life that was once validated to me in a conversation prompted by the wisdom of my own son. My husband wasn't home yet, and my other two children were out with their friends when my son went over to the television, turned it off, and said, "Mom, now that we're alone, I want to talk to you." Uh-oh! I couldn't imagine what was coming. After all, he was fifteen! My heart was in my throat. He began, "Mom…I don't think you're being hard enough on us." What? My mind raced. He continued, "The house would be a lot neater if you made us follow through when you ask us to do something." I thought about the previous couple of weeks, letting them go to the movies even when they hadn't completed their chores as promised; still allowing their friends to come in, when I had said they couldn't have someone over until their rooms were acceptable for guests. In fact, I had warned them on several occasions they couldn't do something if they hadn't read for thirty minutes, or done their homework, or fed the dog. But it dawned on me that on too many occasions lately, it was just easier to do it myself rather than having to ask them over and over and over…(except the homework!).

"You know what, honey," I replied, "you're right." The conversation went on from there, but the gist of it was I agreed with him. I had gotten a bit lax in following through on my minor "demands"…and they were taking advantage of it. After discussing it with my husband, we had a meaningful family discussion on the responsibilities that came with the good fortune of living in a nice home, and that they needed to have more respect for it. After all, they lived here, too, and their friends visited here, too!

The following week was Thanksgiving, and the whole family had worked hard in preparation for company coming both on Thanksgiving Day and on the following day (for the wonderful leftovers!). Unfortunately, I became sick the evening of Thanksgiving and went to bed early after the festivities. I lay in bed wondering how in the world I would get everything done in time for the second round of guests, who would be at our doorstep early the next day. My husband, being too tired to think about it said, "We'll worry about it in the morning." I fell asleep to the sound of dishes clanking, thinking someone was after another piece of pie...

The next morning brought a very pleasant surprise, however! Dane, my middle son (and personal hero of the day), had cleared the table, cleaned the kitchen, and picked up the rest of the house before he went to bed! The relief of having it done was glorious, but the pride my husband and I felt in the fact that he had seen the need to get it done... and gone ahead and taken care of it himself, with no prodding, was the best feeling of all. Just remember: When you make a good point to your children, it really does set in, and is often illustrated in their behavior in ways you had not even dreamed of.

As I said in the first paragraph, my hesitancy in adding a chapter on discipline was because I wanted to concentrate on the nurturing, positive, caring aspects of parenthood. Ironically, these exact words were used in the definition of discipline written in one of the best articles I have ever read on the subject, entitled: Guidance of Effective Discipline, written by the committee on Psychosocial Aspects of Child and Family Health, for the American Academy of Pediatrics. The article began:

> The word discipline, which comes from the root word disciplinare—to teach or instruct—refers to the system of teaching and nurturing that prepares children to achieve competence, self-control, self-direction, and caring for others. An effective discipline system must contain three vital elements: 1) a learning environment characterized by positive, supportive parent-child relationships; 2) a strategy for systematic teaching and strengthening of desired behaviors (proactive); and 3) a strategy for decreasing or eliminating undesired or ineffective behaviors (reactive). Each of these components needs to be functioning adequately for discipline to result in improved child behavior.

This chapter will offer ideas on how to teach your children the value of respect, and the necessity of discipline. In addition, it will offer ways to encourage them to show respect for you, the rest of the family, their friends, and themselves. The hope is that this depth of understanding will lead to a lesser amount of severe discipline. As I stated previously, every child needs boundaries...with appropriate consequences when those boundaries are pushed. Remind your children frequently that discipline and setting rules are forms of love, because you care so much about them you want them to be safe, have bright futures, have lots of good friends, be happy, and be successful throughout their lives.

The goal of parental discipline is to develop self-discipline in the child.

—The Parenting Guild
TheFunPlace.com

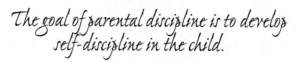

Remember, discipline is different than punishment, and is logically related to the situation. If your child throws a toy on the ground, tell them you are putting it away to keep it safe, until they can show more respect for it.

Let your child be the disciplinarian through playing a game with their stuffed animals. For example, you be the bear and start to "walk" off the bed. Help your child to "teach" the bear that if he goes any further he will fall and hurt himself, rather than "punish" the bear by yelling at him and scaring him! Then, equate that situation to your rule of not playing in the street...because you don't want them to get hurt, either!

If the child is behaving in an unacceptable manner, give a positive alternative. If the child is restless or overactive in the house, suggest outdoor play to run off some energy.

Remember to save your discipline for the important things. A continual bombardment of "no's," make all of them seem inconsequential. When you have to say no, try to find something you can say yes to soon after.

The Magic of Respect...The Secret of Discipline

Make sure your child understands the rules, and then BE CONSISTENT.

❧

Always do your best to treat your children the way you would like to be treated. How would you feel if your boss yelled at you to get you to complete a report for him? Would his attitude motivate you to do it? When you want your child to do something, ask nicely. He will be more likely to obey your request, and will have more respect for you.

❧

In all you do and say, help your children to feel good about themselves. Children (as well as adults!) with a good self-image, usually want to act properly and will try to learn what is expected of them.

❧

LISTEN to your child's explanation of what happened before you react, if you think he has done something wrong—and trust your child before making an assumption. I'll never forget one time when I had told my son to practice the "7s" in his times tables. Within minutes, I heard him playing his guitar! I started to yell up the stairs for him to stop playing and start memorizing, when that little voice inside of me suggested I go up the stairs to check it out first. Midway up I heard him singing, "Seven times seven is forty-nine...seven times seven is forty-nine; seven times eight is fifty-six...YEA...seven times eight is fifty-six" to a tune that he was making up as he went along! I was flabbergasted...and extremely relieved I hadn't yelled at him before I saw how creatively he was trying to learn!

❧

Show your children how to make amends when they make a mistake.

❧

Mommy Magic
Adria Manary

The following story was written by Patricia Schulz's son, when he was fourteen.
It beautifully and innocently illustrates a child's respect and concern for his mother
—something we all wish for!

Respecting Mom's Dream

—by Nick Schulz

My family's "Westward Ho" reached its emotional peak when my mom was finally able to bike through Zion National Park. It all began when she shared her dream with the rest of the family while planning our summer vacation. Biking is my mom's favorite pastime, but none of us had any idea that this family trip would turn into the adventure of our lives!

We started in glitzy Las Vegas, which is where we could have spent our entire vacation if it had been up to my brother and me, but we joined in on our mother's enthusiasm and harnessed her dream in our hearts. We were off to take on the bike trail at Zion in Schulz style—exploring places where few would dare to go!

It was all coming together for my mom. We arrived at Zion National Park late in the day and before even visiting the Visitor Center or doing a quick ride to a scenic overlook, we went directly to the bike rental shop to secure our bikes for the next day. We were all looking forward to a full day of biking along and through the ancient and beautiful Virgin River.

Morning arrived, and all too soon we were outside on our mountain bikes—making the final adjustments, tailoring our seats, setting the gears and loading up with provisions. Finally, we were off! We got as far as the "Welcome to Zion National Park" sign where we took our family photo, hopped back on our bikes and in less than 100 yards, my mom ran right into a huge cactus plant and fell to the ground! She was covered with cactus needles...up and down her legs and on the palms of both hands. The blood was pouring out—but she still had that determined look on her face, so we realized we needed to be her encouragement now. Borrowing her enthusiasm, we helped her up and removed most of the needles. She quickly recovered from the day's first glitch and we biked on.

Going from a four thousand foot elevation to an exasperating eight thousand feet was our next glitch to overcome. As the air became thinner, we pumped harder, none of us wanting to show the other that the elevation was taking the wind out of our sails. We just kept on pushing, silently wishing we had all brought portable oxygen tanks. We knew we could make it—especially with the knowledge that the return trip would be downhill.

We were out of breath and starving by the time we reached the lodge. We were also a bit more realistic about what we had undertaken. Mom decided that she didn't need the ton of cargo on her back, so she took the available shuttle back to our hotel to offload her gear for the return trip. Our cooperation and respect had created a change of heart in Mom too, as far as communing only with nature the entire trip. When she returned from the hotel, she had our walkmans, knowing that music would be an encouraging companion as we took to the trail to continue the steady climb.

So there we were—reenergized and back on the trail—when suddenly my handlebars disengaged! Seeing my mom deflated after realizing that there was no way of fixing them, I told her that all those

Mommy Magic
Adria Manary

years of biking with no hands was sure going to pay off now! "Hey mom," I said. "We are not going to let a little thing like biking uphill with no hands stop the glory of this ultimate bike experience are we?" Mom's glow of happiness as I persevered was my invisible navigation to press on.

Because of our various delays, we arrived at the end of the trail a bit late to take on the "must do" hiking trail, Zion Narrows. The park closed at dusk. At this point, Jackson and I were determined to see this through, so we reminded our parents that we were all power walkers and, this trek would be a piece of cake. We pressed on with vigor through the river gorge, repeating in our heads, "Dusk is coming, dusk is coming." We walked alongside and then in the Virgin River, with the water sometimes thigh high. The rocks were very slippery, so we used a drifting log as an aid. We all had the sense of being tiny specks against the frame of the enormous mountains—and we were all determined to beat time and get back to our bikes for the return trip. The hike was awesome and quick, but the sun would be setting soon. One ranger recommended that we return by shuttle and at first I was relieved thinking that this was authority speaking and so we had to do as we were told... right? Wrong. The look on mom's face once again revived our determination, so we declined the plush ride and got back on our bikes. At least I had working handlebars thanks to this ranger, and another ranger offered words of encouragement saying that the downhill ride would be a breeze and we would probably beat the shuttle to the bottom.

However, it was not a breeze at all...it was more like a tornado! For some strange reason, out of nowhere, Mother Nature charged a windstorm up the canyon. Riding downhill into the wind of resistance made breathing difficult and guiding our bikes almost impossible. In typical Schulz style however, we overcame the odds and made it to the bottom in one piece. We did it! Mom's dream had become a family dream, and although the unpredictable met us at every turn, we accomplished the quest together.

That trip brought our family together for a special memory we will share for the rest of our lives. The rest of our vacation was awesome too, but that day, with all of its little glitches and still making sure mom's dream came true, was by far the best.

Ice Cream Please

It's awful being sick
UNLESS you are a child!
For that is when your every wish
Is granted, no matter how wild!

"Ice cream—please, then Jell-O,
That is what I want
For breakfast, lunch and dinner!"
To the store the mother jaunts.

"This is a magic potion!"
The mother says with hope,
That the little mouth will open
So the "meds" can help them cope.

Fluffy pillows, more TV,
Yummy treats and mom's caress.
Though the body may be aching—
The attention is the BEST!

Being sick isn't so bad when you have a mommy.

—Tommy
(four years old)

Mommy Magic
Adria Manary

Magic Potions for Sick Children

*P*owerful lessons in compassion are ingrained in children from an early age, when they experience the tender devotion and caring of their mother when they are not feeling well. Cinnamon toast and tea come immediately to my mind when I think back on the days of my childhood when a sore throat, cough and stuffy nose would keep me home from school. Ah yes, those uncomfortable yet cozy days on the couch, propped up on fluffy pillows, a Kleenex box by my side, and the television tuned in to "I Love Lucy" reruns. I even remember one time when my brother made my Barbie and Ken dance on the back of the couch to make me laugh—a rare and appreciated performance!

Best of all, of course, was that my mom was by my side constantly. Of course when the illness is more serious, it's no fun for anybody. However, even then, the show of love and concern can provide a sense of warmth and love that will last a lifetime. I can remember being extremely ill as a teenager and every time I opened my eyes, my mom was right there, sometimes sleeping, but always RIGHT THERE. Nobody likes being sick, but at least for a child, the experience can be one of reassurance that they are the most important person in the world, and making them feel better is the absolute top priority for their mom! The hectic pace of the world stops, and the child is shown in no uncertain terms that their well-being ranks above anything else.

I truly believe the acts of compassion we show our children when they are sick are valuable lessons of love. One time when a bird flew into the large glass window in the back of our house, my little boy wanted to bring it in, put it on a pillow and feed it Jell-O. Then he said, "Oh Mommy, he's HURT! Let's make him comfy and rub his head."

Probably the best "potion" for a sick child is being curled up in mom's lap, nestled in her love—but I hope the ideas in this chapter will help to comfort your children when you have to get up to make the Jell-O.

Mommy Magic
Adria Manary

One should not stand at the foot of
a sick person's bed, because that place
is reserved for the guardian angel.

—Jewish Folk Saying

Have a special "feel better" snuggly (a pillow, stuffed animal or something soft) on hand when your child is sick or feeling blue. Keep it in a special place for whenever they need it.

Tell your child that whatever part of their body is hurting, you're feeling the same hurt in yours, because you truly "hurt" for them.

Hold your child's hand and tell them to squeeze it every time it hurts and you will send your special healing through the palm of your hand.

A child usually does not want to stay in bed (unless they are extremely ill) because they feel isolated in their room. Make an especially fluffy, comfy bed on the couch near you—or if they must stay in a bed a distance away, give them a special bell to ring for whenever they need you.

Have all of the family members make special cards for the sick child.

Magic Potions for Sick Children

Always play their favorite quiet game with them.

A hot water bottle (not too hot!) is always comforting
 (Unless they have a fever!)

Help them make a list of fun things they are going to do when they
get well and write down your best guess for when they'll be able
to start doing the things on the list.

Make stuffed animals talk, telling your child little stories
about when "they" were sick.

Make them hot tea and cinnamon toast—or whatever makes them
feel warm and yummy. Whatever you choose, serve it
EVERY TIME they are under the weather.
It provides a wonderful warm and fuzzy memory of comfort.

If no one has called to see how they are, call a couple of relatives
and friends without your child knowing, and ask them to call back
to ask how your child is doing and let your child speak with them.

Remember—laughter is still the best medicine! Rent a funny movie,
let the tickle monster attack, or put a diaper on your head.
Do whatever it takes to get a smile out of your precious little patient.

Mommy Magic
Adria Manary

A soothing song can brighten the day for a sick child. The following story was an extreme yet wonderful case in point...

Like any good mother, when Karen finds out another baby is on the way, she does what she can to help her three-year-old son, Michael, prepare for a new sibling. They find out the new baby is going to be a girl, and day after day, night after night, Michael sings to his sister in Mommy's tummy.

The pregnancy progresses normally for Karen, an active member of the Panther Creek United Methodist Church in Morristown, Tennessee. Then the labor pains come. Every five minutes...every minute. But complications arise during delivery. Hours of labor. Would a C-section be required? Finally, Michael's little sister is born. But she is in serious condition. With siren howling in the night, the ambulance rushes the infant to the neonatal intensive care unit at St. Mary's Hospital, Knoxville, Tennessee. The days inch by. The little girl gets worse. The pediatric specialist tells the parents, "There is very little hope. Be prepared for the worst." Karen and her husband contact a local cemetery about a burial plot. They have fixed up a special room in their home for the new baby, now they plan a funeral.

Michael keeps begging his parents to let him see his sister. "I want to sing to her," he says.

Week two in intensive care. It looks as if a funeral will come before the week is over. Michael keeps nagging about singing to his sister, but kids are never allowed in intensive care. But Karen makes up her mind. She will take Michael whether they like it or not. If he doesn't see his sister now, he may never see her alive.

She dresses him in an oversized scrub suit and marches him into ICU. He looks like a walking laundry basket, but the head nurse recognizes him as a child and bellows, "Get that kid out of here now! No children are allowed in ICU." The mother rises up strong in Karen, and the usually mild-mannered lady glares steel-eyed into the head nurse's face, her lips a firm line. "He is not leaving until he sings to his sister!"

Karen tows Michael to his sister's bedside. He gazes at the tiny infant losing the battle to live. And he begins to sing. In the pure-hearted voice of a three-year-old, Michael sings:

"You are my sunshine, my only sunshine, you make me happy when skies are gray..."

Instantly the baby girl responds. The pulse rate becomes calm and steady. Keep on singing, Michael.

"You'll never know, dear, how much I love you. Please don't take my sunshine away..."

The ragged, strained breathing becomes as smooth as a kitten's purr.

Keep on singing, Michael.

"The other night, dear, as I lay sleeping, I dreamed I held you in my arms..."

Michael's little sister relaxes as rest, healing rest, seems to sweep over her.

Tears conquer the face of the bossy head nurse. Karen glows.

"You are my sunshine, my only sunshine. Please don't take my sunshine away."

The girl is well enough to go home!

Woman's Day magazine called it "The miracle of a brother's song." The medical staff just called it a miracle. Karen called it a miracle of God's love. A few weeks later, Michael's little sister was baptized at the Panther Creek Church.

"I Couldn't Love You More If I Tried"

—by Suzan Schweizer

All of my memories of Mom are enveloped by her constant, un-conditional, never-failing love. I actually had trouble adjusting to life as I entered school and found—to my confusion and hurt—that everyone didn't love me unconditionally.

Her love manifested itself in many ways, one of which was her warm and loving care when I was sick. In fact, being sick was a treat in our home. I actually felt guilty and questioned if I was really sick at times or just looking for the comfort and cocooning that my parents always gave. Mother would always make me a nice warm bath, and afterwards she would have fresh sheets right out of the dryer. I would crawl into bed and lie on the bottom sheet as she "made the bed" right on top of me, letting the top sheet gently float down in a comforting caress. Then came the cosseting of milk toast with sugar, 7-Up, sherbet, custard, Jell-O...in other words, anything I wanted. I remember her saying, "I couldn't love you more if I tried." Her love was the best medicine of all!

Mommy Magic
Adria Manary

Life Goes On

Life is full of tragedy
But hearts are made to heal.
The key to peace is coming back
From life's difficult ordeals.

A child's sweet soul is tender
To be treated gingerly.
Yet it is also given strength
In times of tragedy.

A mother's heart lends comfort—
Her hand, security.
Her confidence in God's wise plan
Gives children certainty…

That life goes on regardless
Of whatever pain is felt—
And that it's up to them to thrive
No matter what they're dealt.

When something bad happens,

hearts open up from all around.

The key is to keep your own heart open

so that the love that comes can heal.

—Adria Manary

Mommy Magic
Adria Manary

Holding on to the Magic When Tragedy Strikes

When tragedy strikes at home, the family glue thickens. Suddenly it's the little things that matter. What doesn't matter is often what mattered most the day before! I believe it is of the utmost importance to include our children in this transition—and to help them understand why things and feelings are changing so dramatically. Whether it is a physical or an emotional crisis, within our immediate family, or within our community of family and friends—our children are affected as much as we are, and oftentimes even more. Therefore, it is also important to let them see how we express our feelings and in turn let them express theirs.

On April 29, 1993, I lost my dear mother to cancer. Ten months later, my dad died of the same cruel and merciless disease. Six months after that my first grandmother passed away. Shortly thereafter, I had to break into my second grandmother's apartment when she would not answer the door...only to find she too had joined the rest of my cherished family in heaven. It didn't end there, however. When we returned home from my grandmother's funeral, we received another dreaded phone call. It was my husband's doctor. The test results were in. Our fears had materialized. He, too, had cancer. The grief I experienced during this period, and beyond, at times seemed insurmountable. The treatment and recovery period for my husband and family at times seemed never-ending. But I was thankfully able to hold on to the magic of the lives that remained—and the life we were now fighting for.

At times I would hide to cry, because I felt my children had experienced enough of the emotions of life. But I was often reminded that they wanted to be there for every tear.

One day I was talking to a friend on the phone and began to cry. Not wanting my five-year-old to see yet another episode of sobbing, I took the phone into the hall and sat on the floor. As I explained to my friend how I longed to hold my mother's hand just one more time, my precious little son came around the corner and put my hand into his. With his other hand he stroked my hair, took my headband off, and tried to relieve the headache I had complained about. He sat there on the floor with me until I got off the phone, and continued to sit there with me in silence until the tears stopped coming. It was the deepest display of compassion I have ever experienced. At the tender age of five, he had soothed my sorrow in a way many adults are not capable of.

It was good for him to have the opportunity to take care of Mommy. At least he could be there and see he could do something to help—rather than be at a friend's home trying to play, while worrying about what was happening at home.

This chapter will gently offer ways to hold on to the magic of being a mother in the midst—and the aftermath—of grave adversity.

Mommy Magic
Adria Manary

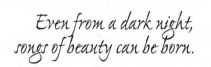

Even from a dark night,
songs of beauty can be born.

—Maryanne Radmacher-Hershey

No one goes through life without the pain of losing someone close to them, dealing with sickness—or one of the many other hurts that life deals us. However, we must always strive to keep looking forward and teach our children to do the same. It was important to me to include this chapter because no one knows when tragedy might strike, and one is never prepared at that moment. So although I pray for the well-being of every reader of this book, I want each of you to know that there is magic here—even in tragedy—when you need it most.

When a death occurs...
- Have the child involved write a letter to that person. It will help to let them communicate things they may not have said, or may still not understand. Read the letter if appropriate, and help them to work through their concerns.
- Let them go to the funeral if they want to. The experience will provide them with some closure.
- Let them choose the flowers they would like to put on the grave or send to the funeral home.
- Encourage them to put something in the casket they've made or something that is special between themselves and the person who died.

- Have pictures at the funeral home of happy moments in the person's life.

❦

When a pregnancy is lost and your children have been aware of the baby, it is important to think of what they have lost as well. Your loving reassurance that they are STILL a big brother or sister, even though their baby is in heaven, will help them cope with the loss and give them something much less scary than the baby just disappearing.

❦

The following may not seem as severe as true tragedy, but in the hearts and minds of children it is probably their first, and therefore gravest tragedy thus far:
- When a pet dies, even the smallest of them, have a proper funeral and burial. Let your child say a prayer and lay flowers on the grave. Please don't flush their dear little goldfish down the toilet.
- When a friend's pet dies, encourage your child to show the proper compassion. Even if it was the neighborhood pet snake that you are glad to be rid of, think of the child who loved it.

❦

Remember your children can't wait. Of course you need time to yourself to grieve or to heal. But your children need you continually. I can remember when my mom passed away, I realized a few months after her death that not only had I lost my mom, but to my dismay... my children were losing their mom. It gave me great reason to find help and cope with my grief in a healthy way that would include my children rather than exclude them.

❦

If someone close to your child has passed away, try reading the following "advice" from the Carmelite Monastery, in Waterford, Ireland. I received this from a friend when my father died and I found it very comforting. In trying to explain why they couldn't see Granddaddy anymore, I also summarized it for my children:

> Death is nothing at all. I have only slipped away into the next room. Whatever we were to each other, that we are still. Call me by my own familiar name. Speak to me in the easy way which you always used to. Laugh as we always laughed at the little jokes we enjoyed together. Play, smile, think of me, pray for me. Let my name be the household word that it always was. Let it be spoken without effort. Life means all that it ever meant, it is the same as it ever was, there is absolutely unbroken continuity. Why should I be out of your mind because I am out of your sight? I am but waiting for you, for an interval, somewhere very near just around the corner. All is well. Nothing is past; nothing is lost. One brief moment and all will be as it was before only better, infinitely happier and forever we will all be one together again.

Although we want to protect our children from the horrors of the world, when something terrible is going on within the household, it is extremely difficult to protect them from the pain of what is happening right around them. Therefore, the best thing we can do for them is to teach them tools to cope. It is important that you do protect them from outsiders who feel they are helping by telling the child too much. Inform those close to you how you want things to be handled with your children. However, sharing feelings with trusted individuals and asking for help is a valuable step in most healing processes. The following is a list of things to watch for in your child that may be signs they are having emotional difficulties:

- trouble concentrating
- crying easily
- eating more or less than usual
- poor grades in school or poor behavior reports from the teacher
- silence—it may seem normal, but it can sometimes be their only cry for help

In the book, *Becky and the Worry Cup*, by Wendy Harpham, she suggests giving your child a worry cup to place their worries in rather than holding them inside. I have heard many versions of this, but whatever you choose, letting your child have an imaginary place to put their worries away can be very helpful, even with everyday life. Simply have them choose a container, and then get pennies, buttons, or something else plentiful and have them explain each worry as they place one of the chosen objects into the container. After they have gone to bed, always empty the container so it can be fresh and ready for another session.

If the tragedy is of another nature, such as the loss of a home in a natural disaster, or having to leave your home abruptly for any other reason, the following may be of assistance:

- If you are getting ready to evacuate, choose one precious item for them to hold.
- Assure them that although things may seem scary, the most important thing is that you stay together as a family. Anything else can be replaced.
- If the worst happens, and there is no home to return to, tell them stories about the many homes you lived in while growing

up and how a "home" is where the family is . . . it doesn't matter where!

⊱

Young children may not be able to express grief or shock the same as an adult can. Encourage them to draw, write or play-act their feelings when you can. They require catharsis as much as any grown-up.

⊱

This is a small list, but a start. Another extremely valuable gift we can bestow upon our children is the ability to always look forward. Despite loss, death, or devastation, life continues to move ahead. Teach them that the "horizon is a wonderful place..." because we never know what is out there waiting for us. Just remember, the best thing we can do for those who depend on us is to simply be there for them...in good times and in bad.

⊱

Holding Grandma's Hand

—by Tamara Amey

When my beloved grandma died after a long and painful illness, it was very hard to say goodbye to her, yet we all agreed it was a blessing to see her relieved of her pain. Grandma required round-the-clock care and we brought her home to live out her remaining days in familiar surroundings. At first, it was difficult deciding how much of this should be shared with our twelve-year-old daughter. As it turned out, Kyla became one of Grandma's caretakers—helping turn her crippled body, rubbing lotion into her dry, fragile skin and even helping change her diapers.

As Grandma took her last breath, surrounded by her family, Kyla was by her side, holding her hand as she passed from this life. She became the parent as she hugged and comforted my father as tears fell from his face. While this was such a painful time for our family, I was very proud of my daughter's maturity and acceptance of this life event. Death is never easy to explain to our children, but letting them share in your grief is a healthy and important step in the healing process. We all miss Grandma very much—but have wonderful memories stored in our hearts by which to remember her. And Kyla will always feel a special part of the final memory that shall be felt in the hearts of the family forever.

Mommy Magic
Adria Manary

Life's Bouquet

I just don't know
Where the mornings go
And especially the afternoons!

Then evening comes
The day is done
And we say goodnight to the moon.

Then it's dawn once more
Dad's out the door
And the day turns into night.

It's happened again
We're in a whirlwind
It's again time to turn out the light!

The sun rises up
Where's my coffee cup?
Liquid energy's on the way!

I take a few sips
Read a book with some tips
And I'm ready to face the day.

But I don't feel the same
As I stare out at the rain
Thankful my husband stayed home.

So I build a nice fire
And then feel inspired
To go in and turn off the phone.

It's time to slow down
And turn things around
Take control of our time and our lives.

Who's stopping me
From feeling free
No one, I realize!

I've just gotten caught up
In this life's daily rut
Starting to drown in the carpool!

So today I'll take hold
As each moment unfolds
And no longer be time's fool.

Mommy Magic
Adria Manary

I feel empowered
Reminded each hour
Is mine to do as I please.

I've locked the world out
and without a doubt
I suddenly feel at ease.

My children walk in
With their fresh shiny grins
With Daddy close behind.

The warmth that they bring
Truly makes my heart sing
I feel such peace of mind.

As I hug each one
I notice the sun
Has chased the rain away.

And made it clear
To always hold dear
The beauty of life's bouquet.

The future of the world would be assured if every child were loved.

—Bernie Siegel

Mommy Magic
Adria Manary

The Precious Present—
The Magic of Changing Your Focus

While writing the update for this book, I found it hard getting started on this chapter. It wasn't writer's block...I think it was "Mommy's block." What I mean is, I was trying to write a chapter on valuing the present, when I was personally caught up in the heartache of realizing how soon my first child would be "leaving the nest," and worries such as, "how are we going to pay college tuition for all four kids!" Making the present your top priority isn't easy sometimes. It is a habit that requires practice and focus, but reaps the greatest benefits.

There is great value in cherishing memories, and it is extremely important to plan for the future, but too often we dwell on one or the other...and that's when it can put a damper on our lives. After experiencing some severe setbacks...I too, have been guilty of letting the past dictate my future, both personally and professionally. The world is not always fair, but it is up to each of us individually to respond positively, and move forward; or accentuate the negative, and not move at all. It is a growth process learning the lessons of life. The question is whether or not we learn from these lessons, always keeping in mind that how we handle them, is how our children will ultimately face their own lessons.

The following quote was taken from the Mystery Lodge Theater in Disneyland, and is one of my favorites because it describes the generational importance of passing on what is in our hearts, as well as what is in our pocketbooks:

If we share the wisdom of our elders with the hearts of our children, life will be full of wonder, spirit and magic.

As I did the research for this book, I not only chatted with over one hundred moms, I also pored through scores of books that I have collected over the years. To my surprise and utter delight, I came upon an old journal of my own, where I was doing my best to pass on what was in my heart. The first page started out as follows:

Adria Manary 4/17/98

Somehow, writing my name and the date on the inside cover of this journal gave me the intuitive feeling that it was already an old and treasured memory. Whoever is reading this now (probably Chase, Dane or Astra)—I hope the memories collected here—and beyond— are wonderfully happy...because that would mean our family's future is bright—which is what I pray for every single day!

At the time, I obviously thought one of my children would be reading it years from now, which most likely will still happen, but little did I know the first person who would pick it up would be me! How thankful I am that my prayers have been answered thus far and what a good lesson it has been to be present with my children, as well as continue to grow with them.

Another one of my breakthrough moments came one day when I took my son to the doctor because his knees had been aching constantly. Ironically, his diagnosis turned out to be a simple case of growing pains! It dawned on me that I, too, had been experiencing different kinds of "growing pains" through the challenges I had faced, but I was now ready for a personal, parental and professional growth spurt!

Whether it is transitioning from pregnancy to the thrill and relief of holding your healthy, miraculous child in your arms; from baby to toddler; from toddler to a "he's not a baby anymore" look; from child to pre-teen; then the big one...adjusting to the teenage years...and then the ultimate...becoming their friend in adulthood...appreciating the present, is a present you can continually give to yourself as well as to your family.

Mommy Magic
Adria Manary

The best thing to spend on your child,
is your time.

–Arnold Glasgow

Take a few moments to hold your children when they wake up each morning. Put the paper down, turn the news off, hang up the phone, whatever you need to do to focus on them to start their day wrapped in a feeling of utter love and security. I recently read about a mother who had quite a rude awakening. As she told it, one morning when her child awakened, he toddled into the living room...still sleepy-eyed.

She looked at him adoringly as he walked across the room, and watched as he reached his arms up high, whimpering in anticipation. As she sadly recalled, her precious child continued to reach up, on his tippy-toes at this point, but he was not reaching up for her to hold him. Instead, he was trying to reach the buttons on the TV set.

Although we feel it is getting harder and harder to find time for anything these days, documented concern over being too busy for our children is almost two centuries old, as evidenced by the following quote:

We are always too busy for our children; we never give them the time or interest they deserve. We lavish gifts upon them; but the most precious gift, our personal association, which means so much to them, we give grudgingly.

–Mark Twain (1835–1910)

At this point in the book, I would like to encourage you to pause for just a moment, close your eyes, think about the past week—and consider how many times your full focus has been on your children. Then, plan how it might be different next week. Turn off the television, computer, cell phone, ipod, or radio often, so that you can concentrate fully—with no interruptions—on what's going on in your child's mind.

Mommy Magic
Adria Manary

―by Andrea Lagassé

It was Christmas time once again, and my husband and I were trying to decide what to get our four children. Had it really been fifteen years since that memorable Christmas when we joyfully realized we had not only become parents, but had also become Mr. and Mrs. Santa Claus? Every family goes through phases, and I wouldn't trade one little squeal of glee from all those wonderful Christmas mornings, but somehow I felt we were ready for a change. I could tell my husband was thinking the same thing. For years we had been talking about how we kept accumulating so much stuff. So many toys, so many gadgets, so many knick-knacks...so many treasures that were now missing pieces, had been played with or worn only once or twice, or were old and forgotten at the bottom of a toy box. It wasn't just the children either; the two of us had plenty of our own stuff... buried in kitchen drawers and closets! This time, however, the conversation led us to a huge revelation that turned last Christmas into one of our very best! As we eventually looked at the famous "wish lists" and adorable letters to Santa, we realized there were no particular items the kids were dying to have; and the things they did want, we knew would end up under a bed or hidden in a closet in a matter of weeks after opening. We just couldn't justify spending money on things that were not going to last much past the New Year, and yet it was Christmas!

At that very moment, the revelation came to us. Let's ask the kids what they would like to DO, instead of what they would like to HAVE! What if they could choose something they had always wanted to do, but time or lack of resources had not allowed it? Eureka! We were on to something new, different, special, wonderful...and then, of course, we wondered if this was something that would appeal to parents only. Much to our surprise, they all had something they were really interested in doing! Now, not only would each of the kids get to do something truly special that they normally wouldn't have done, but it would give us the rare opportunity to spend very special one parent-one child time together.

Jill was fifteen and said she dearly wanted to go with me to an opera in Seattle. Neither of us had ever gone to one, so the excitement mounted for both of us. The choice was Carmen and we ordered the tickets. We both had fun reading about the history of the opera, what people wear, and how one is supposed to act during a performance. Since I didn't want to completely break the tradition of opening presents, I found a CD set with a book explaining the whole opera. Jill was able to read about it and listen to the music before we went, which tripled her enthusiasm. I wrapped up the tickets, CDs, and book to be opened Christmas morning.

On her special day, Jill and I started off early. We began with a mocha from Starbucks and then spent the day shopping together. Lunch was a feast of food and conversation...and finally, that evening, we experienced the opera. It was even more awesome than we had expected! The surroundings, the people, the clothes, the music, the

Mommy Magic
Adria Manary

performances...in Jill's words, "It was too cool." We even rented those tiny binoculars so we could see every detail. We could not get the smiles off our faces as we drove home. I took lots of pictures that I put into a photo album for her to vividly remember her Christmas present from 2003. She has thanked me over and over and says how she will never forget it. She also loves telling the whole story to her friends—which for a fifteen-year-old girl, is a major sign of joy!

Jeff was twelve and immediately knew what he wanted to do...ride go-karts! He and Dad left early to spend the whole day together, just as Jill and I had done. They started at the glass museum in Tacoma and then went to the racetrack, where instructors taught the kids all the rules and then tested them on the track. Jeff passed the class and proudly received his certificate and "license." He bought a cool race hat, and Darrin took pictures of him having an absolute blast racing around the track. After that, they went to lunch and then stopped at a Harley-Davidson shop. They sat on motorcycles and dreamed together, as my husband's "inner child" came out to play, too. They ended the day with a movie and came home with the true feeling of Christmas in their hearts...joy. The smile on Jeff's face when he got home and the excitement in his voice as he relived the day for us, let me know our instincts were correct—this was indeed the best Christmas gift yet. I put the pictures of his special day into an album like Jill's, which he proudly shows to anyone who will look at it with him!

Brandon was eight and wanted to see the motorcycle races at the Tacoma Dome. Waiting was the hardest and longest for him, since his Christmas present wasn't realized for three months, but his anticipation and excitement brought many opportunities to have special talks with Dad about the very exciting day they would be spending together. From Christmas morning until the event, he would bring out the pictures we had wrapped up for him, and talk about the "flying" motorcycles!

The morning of his Christmas event came and Darrin could finally wake Brandon with the words he had been longing to hear, "Today's your day!" Brandon jubilantly put on his Army pants and he and Dad left early, heading straight to the military surplus store. In addition to being a big motorcycle enthusiast, he is also a fan of the military. Darrin took lots of pictures of Brandon wearing camouflage, holding rifles, and even wearing a gas mask. His grin was huge! After a morning filled with Army dreams, Darrin and Brandon headed to Burger King for lunch, Toys "R" Us for the afternoon, and McDonalds for dinner—making it obvious who was in charge!

Watching motorcycle stunts and races at the dome that evening was truly the icing on the cake. If that wasn't enough, they got to go into the "pit" area where Brandon got to meet many of the motorcycle riders. They were true "Christmas angels," giving autographs and letting him sit on their motorcycles! Talk about memories! Even though Darrin's "inner child" emerged once again, he remembered to take the necessary pictures that made Brandon's album the talk of the neighborhood.

Our youngest child, Andrew, was a cheerful six-year-old, who kept Santa very much alive in his wish. He also got what every child wants at Christmas—he received his present EARLY! He wanted to ride on the Santa Train that runs from Snoqualmie to North Bend, and I must admit I was thrilled to keep the tradition of a visit to Santa! He and I started out the day at IKEA. We ate lunch at McDonald's (his favorite, of course) and then had loads of fun riding the train, eating cookies, drinking hot chocolate and sitting on Santa's lap at the train station. I bought Andrew a really cute toothbrush, a snowglobe, and a puzzle, which I wrapped up and put under the Christmas tree for him. I kept my camera busy once again, getting great shots of him next to many different trains, people dressed in train outfits, and even a marine in uniform collecting Toys for Tots. I bought him a little train that ran

Mommy Magic
Adria Manary

on batteries that he played with for the rest of the day...and, by the way, has still not ended up lost under his bed! We went to the mall afterwards and split a pizza and a Cinnabon. His favorite part was watching them make the Cinnabons, which I also took a picture of. He rode on the carousel and then fell asleep as we drove home in the dark after a simply delightful day. I was able to get the pictures developed and into his special album prior to Christmas morning, which he unwrapped along with the train memorabilia. He was SO excited all over again and he, too, loves showing anyone who will look at his special train album, with all of the memories of our day together. There have been many afternoons when I have found him sitting contentedly, looking through his pictures, reliving his special Christmas gift.

This had to have been our most fun gift-giving time for our children, and one we now intend to do each year, if possible. The memories and bonds we built together not only lasted into the new year, but I'm sure they will last for a lifetime! One of the greatest benefits was my husband and I being able to spend one-on-one time with each child, appreciating and enjoying their unique little worlds. Their guards were down and they shared their hearts and dreams with us in a way that cannot be duplicated in a group. It was their day and they got to choose where we went and what we did. Not only did they feel special, they also felt deeply treasured and valued by us. Toys and games are fun, but time spent together—talking, laughing, and doing something that your child really wants to do—is an intangible gift that can never get lost in a toy box.

Mommy Magic
Adria Manary

A Mother's Bond

Holding her close
Her heart touching mine
All I could think
Was, "Oh how divine."

No greater a love
Could there ever be
No stronger a bond
Than between her and me.

The feelings that flowed
From my heart, mind and soul
Enlightened my spirit
As we again became whole.

A mother and child
From conception are one
And together they stay
Until life is done.

Though disjoined at birth
Their soul-flow connection
Remains through their lives
With the deepest affection.

Forever united
Rhythmic in heart
A child and its mother
Are never apart.

I think Dr. Benjamin Spock said it best...

What good mothers and fathers instinctively feel like doing for their babies, is usually best after all.

Mommy Magic
Adria Manary

15

The True Magic
of a Mother's Intuition

*H*ave you ever picked up the phone to call your mother, and her voice is saying "hello" before you push the first button of her number? Have you ever awakened in the middle of the night only seconds before your child cried out for you? Have you ever experienced the feeling something was wrong with your child—and when you investigated, found you had arrived in the nick of time to stop the disaster? Has your child ever brought you something you were just looking for?

For years I have had things like these happen, but hadn't researched the validity of it. In performing the research for this book, however, I found many studies had been performed in this area—with amazing stories and results. Some call it maternal instinct, which is easier for people to accept for some reason. I call it a gift from God. But call it what you may, it is a phenomenon that has occurred generation after generation after generation.

I wanted to end this book discussing this subject because I feel it is the true magic every mother can call upon from the depths of her soul. If you would like to enjoy a truly fascinating book on the subject,

I would suggest the book, A Mother's Link, by Cassandra Eason. As a Fellow at the Alister Hardy Research Center for Religious Experience in Oxford, England, she has studied the subject thoroughly and offers a grand variety of compelling stories in her book.

When my own daughter Astra was only three years old, she proved to me we indeed have a very special "link." One evening while we were on vacation in Southern California, we all sat watching a movie, pleasantly exhausted after a fun-filled day of swimming and sightseeing. I was sitting on the floor thinking of my mother who had passed away four years earlier and how much I missed her. I stared blankly at the movie thinking about how I wished she could have been with us that day and how she never even saw Astra. Out of the blue, Astra walked over to me, cupped my face in her little hands and said, "Don't worry Mommy, your mommy is okay." Tears filled my eyes and she hugged me as if she had become the mother and I the child. Whether she read my thoughts, or my mom had sent her a message to relate to me doesn't matter. Whatever the reason those precious words came out of her mouth, I was deeply thankful for the comfort they brought.

In A Mother's Link there are many stories of how a mother saved her child's life by realizing there was danger only seconds before it happened. One such story told by a mother in Salt Lake City, Utah goes as follows:

>...I felt an especially close bond with my second daughter Sarah and was told by family that we were too close. One evening when she was about eight months old I was in the kitchen, and Sarah and her sister Monica were in the living room with my husband. Suddenly I had a terrible feeling. I rushed to the living room where my husband was reading and Monica was playing. The baby was lying in the corner on her stomach, apparently quite happy. However, when I flipped her over to pick her up, I saw that she was silently choking on a balloon. My husband and Monica were not aware of the emergency!

Mommy Magic
Adria Manary

In this extreme case, as well as thousands of others, it is obvious that mothers' intuition is alive and well and living in every home where children dwell. The trick is to key into it in everyday levels of activity. I would sincerely like to encourage you to listen to your own heart when it concerns your child. Only you know what is truly best for your children. All you have to do is be quiet and listen...the answers will come from within.

This is the only chapter where only one idea is offered, because you have all of the answers you need, right at your fingertips. I simply suggest you take at least five minutes a day to sit quietly and listen to that little voice we all have inside of us. The answers and ideas that will come from the depths of your spirit will enlighten you, especially when you need them most. Listen to this guidance, follow it and trust it...and your journey through motherhood will be enhanced by an angel's care.

Mommy Magic
Adria Manary

A Special Heart Connection

—by Suzan Schweizer

When I was about ten years old, my mother shocked me with her keen intuition. My brother Larry was returning home from Korea, and the whole family was anxiously awaiting his arrival. That morning my father headed down to the supply store where he often traded. As he entered the store, several of the men were obviously in a serious discussion. Seeing my father as he came through the door, one of the men said, "Did you hear? One of our planes that was returning to the States just went down. The reports say a lot of our servicemen were aboard. Sad thing they made it through the war and now..."

My father stopped abruptly, as though he'd hit a brick wall. "Larry!" That's all he could say before he collapsed. The other men helped him up off the floor and brought him around. As soon as he recovered from the initial shock of hearing what had happened and that it was the flight his son was expected on, he called home. "Don't send Suzan to school. I'll be right home. I'll explain when I get there." Of course my mom greeted him outside as he drove into the driveway.

He gently explained the circumstances and that Larry was listed as a passenger when suddenly Mother said, "Larry isn't on that plane! I can't tell you how I know, but he is NOT on that plane!" Five minutes after that, Larry called! We rejoiced like we have never rejoiced before or since. He had been trying to get through to us to let us know he had indeed missed that plane and knew we would be sick with worry. Little did he know that he HAD gotten through to our mother!

I could hardly believe my mother's telepathic ability at the time, but having been a mother now for over thirty years, I look back on the many times where I, too, have used this God-given capability. Maybe not in such dramatic illustrations, but certainly in situations where I have been needed. I can hardly count the times when I have called my own daughters and they've answered the phone with, "How do you always know when I need to talk with you?"

During the aftermath of the tragic earthquake in Turkey in August of 1999, I read an amazing story of a man who succeeded in finding his mother in the rubble after a dream he had about her. In the dream, his mother called to him saying, "Son, please help me. I'm here." He awakened, knowing his mother was alive when everyone else had given up hope. He had already lost his son in the earthquake and his father had been hospitalized, so he was NOT going to give up on finding his mother. The odds against finding her were worsened by the fact that she could not walk or talk, due to a stroke. As they dug through the ruins, the rescuers tried to convince him gently that there was little hope. He badgered them to keep searching. Then he heard a humming noise—the only noise his mother was able to make. It led him to his mother and his dream came true.

Our sensitivity, our "mommy antennas," are up and quivering throughout our lifetimes for however we need to use them. It is indeed a gift to be cherished.

About the Author

Adria Hilburn Manary is a writer, poet, professional speaker, and work-at-home mom. Pictured above with her husband Joel and their precious children—Chase, Astra, Dane and Josh, they all absolutely love living near the beach in sunny San Diego!

Adria has a unique blend of talents, which she now devotes to helping women across the globe to reach their highest potential, while giving back to the world. She is the author of four books and a contributing author to five other titles.

As the mother of four, with degrees in Psychology and Communications, her practical tips, as well as her encouraging words, come from hands on experience as well as research. Adria has made appearances on national television shows, including MSNBC as a parenting expert, as well as many local talk shows, such as Good Morning Oregon and Fox Morning News. She has also been featured on radio and in many newspapers and magazines around the world.

Adria is excited about this new book series, as she believes that the "magic" of life is all around us, but we are often too busy to enjoy or enhance it for ourselves and others. Therefore, her goal in the series is to offer tips, tricks and inspiration on how to live life to the fullest, by living out our purpose joyfully and successfully.

After earning her degrees from Virginia Polytechnic Institute and State University, Ms. Manary started her career as the first woman on the marketing communications team at Westinghouse Corporation Headquarters. One of the projects that she helped to create and execute won the Gold Award at the New York TV and Film Festival. After leaving Westinghouse, she became the Director of Development for New York Special Olympics, where she raised over a million dollars for their programs.

Adria moved back to Washington to marry and decided to try real estate, where she became the rookie of the year and sold an actual castle! Throughout all of her career changes however, she never stopped writing, which is her true passion. After having her first precious baby, she decided to live out her dream of writing for a living—partly because of her passion and mostly because she could not bear the thought of leaving her child! Since that decision, she has had two more beautiful children, adopted another and became a best selling author.

While living in the nation's capital, Adria created and published the entertaining newspaper, Washington Fun Times, The Alternative to Bad News! She also co-wrote the lyrics and melodies for her family music

CD, Precious Souls; created the Magic Whispers® Pillow; and is the co-founder of the Mommy Magic Kids Club online. Although Adria is a woman of many talents who has held many impressive titles, her favorite and most important title will always be, "Mom!"

The smiles of inspiration behind the original *Mommy Magic*, published in 2000

Mommy Magic
Adria Manary

Story Contributors

Val Acciani is a the proud mother of two boys...actually now young men. A native Californian she enjoys designing clothes and teaching water aerobics.

Tamara Amey is an ambitious and caring mom who shares her parenting skills and feelings with other mothers on the "Net." As manager of the ParentsPlace.com newsletter, she updates valuable information every week for its many subscribers who enjoy it.

Letitia Baldrige is America's best-selling author of books on manners, business conduct and human behavior. Her books have sold in the millions. She has had a distinguished career in government and business, having served in the American embassies in Paris and Rome and in the White House, as chief of staff to Jacqueline Kennedy. Letitia Baldrige's More Than Manners: Raising Today's Kids to Have Kind Manners and Good Hearts, is a really wonderful addition to every parent's library.

Sandi Bruegger lives in St. Louis, Missouri with her husband John and daughters, Madison and Skyler. She feels blessed to be a "stay-at-home" mom.

Anne Rogers Gallant was born and raised in Mobile, Alabama, and considers herself a true daughter of the South. After leaving her beloved Alabama to pursue a career in dance in Southern California, she returned home briefly to aid Vietnam War hero Jeremiah Denton in his successful campaign for the United States Senate. She then served for six years in the Senate in Washington, D.C. as a staff assistant to Senator Denton. She currently resides in Fairfax Station, Virginia with her husband Karl, and devotes her full time and energy to the magic of being a mother to sons Karl Jr. and Peirson.

Andrea Lagassé has been married to her wonderful husband Darrin, for thirty years. She homeschooled all four of their children: Jill, Jeff, Brandon and Andrew, always making sure that their energetic dog, Taylor, never ate the homework! She and her family live on JOY Lane, enjoying five acres of Scotchbroom and Christmas trees. "I just love being involved in my church, family and children's lives. Not even spending three years living in Germany and traveling throughout Europe, compares to the simple joys of being a mom!"

Terry Lieberstein provides innovative, interactive nature programs for kids of all ages. She has a Master's Degree in Physical Geography and is also an accomplished folk singer and songwriter. Terry's CD entitled *Turkey Burps and T-Ball* is filled with fun, singable songs that are enjoyed by kids and adults alike.

Mommy Magic
Adria Manary

Jeanette Lisefski is the proud mother of three fantastic children and the founder of At-Home Mother Magazine and the National Association of At-Home Mothers.

Nicholas Schulz is not only a writer, but also a very accomplished soccer player. In his youth he played on the Vienna Arsenal Club Soccer Team for about nine years. In high school he played all four years, lettering in soccer in his senior year. His freshmen year in college he was recruited to play soccer for Shepherd University, Division 2 RAMS soccer team, completing the season in the top twenty-fifth in the nation for Division 2 teams. His hobbies include deejaying parties, dancing, biking, hiking, and watching movies. Oh yes, he especially loves "cruising," thanks to his grandparents family tradition.

Patricia Rovis Schulz (Trish) and her son, Nicholas, are quite a duo! Along with her husband, Rick, and youngest son, Jackson, they have created special family times that could fill a separate book! One of their many wonderful traditions began before Jackson was born. Twenty five years ago, Trish's grandmother, Nonie, passed away. Although the entire family felt a tremendous void in her absence, she had secured a plan that would continue to make them happy for years after her departure from this life. She had set up what she called a "Fun Fund"—a trust fund only to be used for family fun. Trish's dad honored his mom's request by taking the entire family (he and his wife, their four children and grandchildren) on a cruise. Every year, for seventeen years, the entire family escaped to paradise aboard a cruise ship filled with fun—thanks to Nonie. When asked for a bio on herself, Trish replied,

"As for me, I'm doing what the Bee Gee's sang so much about, "STAYIN' ALIVE!" Aside from enjoying the greatest gift of all, being a parent to my BOYS, my other pastimes include: substitute teaching, especially loving the little first graders; jewelry making; songwriting; producing slide shows; and traveling!"

Suzan Schweizer is the mother of three wonderful children, and is blessed with six terrific grandchildren. Looking back at her child rearing days, she feels that her biggest accomplishment was in handling the difficulties of being a career Navy wife. Being creative, nurturing and loving her three children through thirteen relocations in twenty-five years has been her greatest challenge in life. She is an avid reader and traveler and loves to write in her spare time. She resides with her husband in Chesapeake City, MD.

Lorena Serna is a happily married mother of a beautiful daughter. Being a military family, they travel extensively, so she has always chosen work that gave her the flexibility to move when necessary, as well as be near to her child.

Linda O'Leary Sheetz is the proud mother of two loving, sensitive and independent-thinking children.

Christine Sumstine is the proud mother of three wonderful sons who fill her life with joy every day. As a community activist in Oceanside, California, she served on many PTA Executive Boards as well as several district wide committees, dedicated to meeting the educational, social, and emotional needs of children and their families. She now resides in Northern California, in a much more laid back community which she enjoys immensely at this point in her life.

Mommy Magic
Adria Manary

Bibliography

Eason, Cassandra. The Mother Link, Berkeley, CA: Seastone, 1999.

Linkletter, Arthur G. Kids Still Say the Darndest Things, New York: Bernard Geis Associates, 1959.

Shaw, Eva. For the Love of Children, Deerfield Beach, FL: Health Communications, 1998.

Internet Resources:
Inspirational Quotes: The Collection
Good Quotations By Famous People
Famous Quotes

Please visit our website
www.TheMagicofLifeSeries.com

Send your stories and comments, enter the contests, utilize the resources, purchace loving gifts, get updates, and find out where Adria is speaking next.

Magic of Life Favorites

A Different Kind of Pillow Talk!

The Magic Whispers Pillow is filled with the love that only YOU can provide for you children or your sweetheart...when you have to be away from them. Record stories or a simple "I love you"—or download their favorite songs. It is a wonderful way to stay connected in these busy times!

Music for the Whole Family

From "The Magic of Love" to "My Little Man", Adria's songs have warmed the hearts of many families. As one mom wrote, "I LOVED *Mommy Magic*, but I didn't know you sang too! You have a beautiful voice and a beautiful soul. My little girl and I listen to you every day!"

The Magic of Life team looks forward to hearing from you soon!

Mommy Magic
Adria Manary

Praise for Mommy Magic

"Mommy Magic *is a blessing and an inspiration...A wealth of fun ideas. I was moved by the touching stories about the true magic that happens when you become a mom!"*

—Kristi Miller, host of Good Morning Central Oregon

"Mommy Magic*...taps the wellspring of wonder often overlooked in the grind of living the adult life. It offers a child-centered, get-down-on-the-floor approach that many parents and caregivers will find refreshing."*

—Parenting magazine

"What you have written is simply wonderful!"

—Phyllis Diller, comedienne

"I think every mother on this planet should have a copy of this book. I'm bringing it with me today to Head Start, to share with the moms and the teachers."

—Patty Moore, Kaila's mom

More Praise for Mommy Magic

"Mommy Magic *Casts a Spell of Love*"

—The Cincinnati Enquirer
Family section front page headline

"We've never had a book signing like yours. It was as though you personally touched the heart of every person there. You went above and beyond with the woman who was grief stricken...I'm not sure how I would have handled that, but you did so beautifully and thoughtfully. The kind and giving way that you deal with people is truly magical. I hope that you will visit us again when Daddy Magic *comes out!"*

—Community Relations Manager
Joseph-Beth Booksellers,
Lexington, Kentucky

"I have just completed reading your book. I am spellbound. I nearly cried when I read your 'Memories of Mom.' Your book shines with magic and beauty. It must be read by mothers and fathers alike."

—Matt Sundakov, New Zealand

"Without a doubt, your book is a hit with all the people who were at the conference, as well as with the guests at the meetings we've been hosting across the country. They can't keep Mommy Magic *on the shelves!"*

—Barbara Jack, Vice President,
Books and Beyond, Inc.

More Praise for Mommy Magic

"I loved Mommy Magic *but when I heard you sing 'The Magic of Love' from your Precious Souls CD, my little girl and I both cried.*"

—Kristie, Tulsa, Oklahoma

"*As a mother of a one-year-old little girl, I have read many, many books and articles on parenting in the past year or so. Your book,* Mommy Magic, *is by far the most touching, inspirational, and idea-filled book that I have come across. It is a huge resource for all mothers. Thank you for making a difference in my life...*"

—Variny, Alexandria, Virginia

"*I was feeling completely overwhelmed by the 24/7 aspect of motherhood. Fortunately, my neighbor gave me your book and I stayed up all night reading it. I can't thank you enough for giving me back the true feeling of what being a mother means, along with the tools I needed to face another day with my three young, adorable, but demanding children!*"

—Lisa, Paramus, New Jersey

"*I didn't know you sang, too! I was so delighted to receive your CD. My son and I listen to you every day! You have a beautiful voice and a beautiful spirit.*"

—Melony, Kansas City, Kansas

"*It made me laugh and it made me cry—but most of all it provided me with a handy reference for those days when my mind just couldn't conjure up another fun-filled, worthwhile activity for my child!*"

—Trisha, Madison's mom

More Praise for Mommy Magic

"I had been in a real Mommy slump lately. This book is so awesome. It just healed me. I am ready to take it all on again today."

—Marie, New York, New York

"Manary weaves touching stories, poems, quotations, and valuable information...for putting a twinkle in the eyes of a child."

—North County Times, San Diego, CA

"Ms. Manary has created an inspiring guide to positive mothering. What made this book such a gem to read was its basis in reality."

—WomanLinks.Com

"Mommy Magic is a breezy compilation of ideas and wisdom that may do what seems impossible: put the fun back into home life...which has become way too chaotic!"

—The Arizona Republic

"Mommy Magic goes beyond most parenting books. It is an inspiring reference—filled with enchanting suggestions, practical tips, heartwarming stories, and fun activities to help you keep the magic alive during the hectic pace of day-to-day parenting."

—www.mommiesontheweb.com